# *Rubicon*

## DEVELOPMENTAL STEPS AGES 7–10

**GA 307** (*Gesamtausgabe*)**, August 11, 1923, Page 136**

The greatest Divine revelation is a developing human being. If one learns to know about growing human beings, not merely the anatomical-physiological aspects, one learns how soul and spirit flow down into the physical body. Then any knowledge of the human being transforms itself into religiosity, into devotional, awed reverence before that which streams into the temporal surface from Divine depths. That is how we receive that which supports and sustains us as teachers and what children already sense, that which becomes dedication and natural authority.

# Rubicon

## Developmental Steps Ages 7–10

### Selections from the Works of Rudolf Steiner

**Compiled by Mona Ruef**

*with texts newly translated from the German
by Nina Kuettel*

*Texts previously translated from Rudolf Steiner Archives
newly edited by Nina Kuettel*

**Verlag Förderstiftung Anthroposophische Medizin
im Verlag am Goetheanum**

*Printed with support from the Waldorf Curriculum Fund*

Published by:

Waldorf Publications at the
Research Institute for Waldorf Education
38 Main Street
Chatham, NY 12037

Title: *Rubicon: Developmental Steps Ages 7–10*
        *Selections from the Works of Rudolf Steiner*
Compiler: Mona Ruef
Translator/Copy editor: Nina Kuettel
Proofreader: Melissa Merkling
Layout: Ann Erwin
© 2014 Waldorf Publications
ISBN #978-1-936367-67-2

Originally published in German
*Rubikon: Eine Sammlung aus den Werken von Rudolf Steiner*
© 2012 Verlag Förderstiftung Anthroposophische Medizin im Verlag
am Goetheanum, CH-4143 Dornach
ISBN #978-3-905791-08-2

Permission to translate and publish in English is granted through
Freie Hochschule für Geisteswissenschaft, Medizinische Sektion

# Table of Contents

*Ordered by date and sequence of the* Gesamtausgabe *(Complete Works)*

## Child Development between Ages 9 and 10

Translator's note: GA excerpts newly translated are so noted [NK]; excerpts from existing translations have been edited. The original translations can be found on the Rudolf Steiner Archive online at http://www.rsarchive.org.

## Advice for Teachers and Educators for Age 9/10

# Teaching Content for the Ninth Year of Life

Nachlassverwaltung, Dornach, Switzerland, 1943. This
eText edition is provided through the work of The Rudolf
Steiner Publishing Co., London.
Pictorial teaching and flexible concepts – Plant studies in
connection with the Earth and Sun forces – The human
being as aggregation of the entire animal world

These lectures form one of the most comprehensive
introductions to the philosophy of Waldorf education.
They have been published under the titles: *Education
and Modern Spiritual Life*, *The New Art of Education*,
and *A Modern Art of Education*. Published in German
as *Gegenwärtiges Geistesleben und Erziehung*, this edition
is presented here with the kind permission of the Rudolf
Steiner Nachlassverwaltung, Dornach, Switzerland, 1943.
This eText edition is provided through the wonderful work
of The Rudolf Steiner Publishing Co., London.
Up to age 9, presentation of plants and animals in a fairytale/
magical way; afterward the study of plants and animals
– Mineralogy, physics, chemistry, and connections to history
and geography at ages 11 and 12 – Languages studies
– The importance of rules of grammar – Introduction of the
Spiritual/Divine in general; The New Testament beginning
from age 9/10

Empathy – Difference between the world and "I"
– Transition lessons from plants to animals – Writing what
is felt

(excerpts from *Human Values in Education*, Anthroposophic
Press, 2004)
Causal definitions after age 12

# Foreword

In this collection of written works, Mona Ruef has, for the first time, assembled the various indications given by Rudolf Steiner about the beginning of preadolescence. Steiner calls this period in a child's development the "Rubicon" because it is during this time that one developmental phase is brought to fulfillment and the maturing person irretrievably leaves behind his or her childhood. It is compared to Julius Caesar's famous crossing of the Rubicon River in 50 BC when he refused to return to Rome and, instead, moved with his army further north.

With this collection, elementary school teachers, special education teachers, therapists, and school physicians have been given the opportunity to quickly and comprehensively inform themselves about this sensitive developmental stage. One finds in this compact work more than methodic/didactic indications, how each particular subject can be oriented toward this Rubicon of child development. It also includes very general aspects, as well as advice for a teacher's own self-development: For example, the insecurity a child faces between ages 9 and 10 requires a special kind of guidance. And, this Rubicon can be crossed without harm to further development only if a child experiences a teacher or other adult individual as someone who stands before him or her in truth and with integrity.

At this age, if a child cannot turn, full of acceptance and with venerable respect, to an adult, he or she will not have the crucial guiding force and inner soul-spiritual resilience needed for further inner development such as can be predisposed through religious training in which feelings like devotion and reverence are fed and nourished. "Therefore, we should establish our education and instruction in such a way that, in the class where children cross the Rubicon, between the ages of 9 and 10, we really stand before them so that, through our own morality, through that which we possess of inner veracity and content of soul, we can really be something to children; not merely have an effect as an exemplary model, but that everything we say will be perceived as truth."

Indifference to the point of disrespect, yes, even contempt for adults, robs maturing human beings of the very necessary inner, straightening force, which, in the end, also has a negative effect on individual and societal health. That which in childhood is veneration for a treasured and loved adult becomes in adolescence reverence for truth and knowledge. If these things have a central place in a child's development, the critical well of strength that is needed to meet the challenges of life is tapped.

In the name of the International Association of School Physicians, of which Mona Ruef has been an engaged member and co-worker for over thirty years, I offer my most heartfelt gratitude for giving us this Rubicon Collection.

– Michaela Glöckler
Goetheanum
Department of Medicine
July 2012

# Introduction

**GA 297, May 21, 1920, Page 193f.**

"The ninth year becomes ( … ) a Rubicon. In inner consciousness, a child loosens from his or her surroundings and differentiates the self from the environment. Children differentiate their own self from the authority of the environment, but offer devotion to it with love."

It has been many years since Annette Himmelstoss, practicing physician and school physician in Nürtingen, Germany, gave me some reading material from the works of Rudolf Steiner on the subject of the second seven-year epoch.

Over time, it has grown into a collection of material on the theme of the Rubicon, the phase in child development with such very important implications for the rest of a person's life. I compiled and edited the writings about this correlation for a school physicians' seminar in Dornach, Switzerland. It contains excerpts from Rudolf Steiner's works that show how he, again and again and from various angles, emphasized this important life stage and the great significance it holds for the rest of a child's life. We are given important indications for the study of plants and animals, teaching natural science and eurythmy, but above all, for sensitive and personal adult/child relationships at this age that can be of help to children for a successful crossing of the "Rubicon."

I hope this collection, which for us adults is also often associated with multifaceted and foundational memories, provides encouragement and motivation as we deal with this special time in children's lives. My sincere thanks go to all those who took part in putting together this collection of written works, especially to Irene Groh, whose help was invaluable.

– Mona Ruef

# Child Development between Ages 9 and 10

**GA 84, April 30, 1923, Page 205**

When children have settled into this necessary, natural feeling of authority one sees how between ages 9 and 10 they go through a kind of crisis. Everything happens at the level of feelings and perceptions; there is no accountability. A child approaches a teacher and wants something in particular. If we wished to clothe it in words, the child would say: Until now everything that was beautiful was beautiful because a teacher held it to be beautiful, and everything that was true was true because a teacher held it to be true.

However, at this point in time, children go through a crisis. They would question: Who justifies this authority before the whole world? How does the teacher know that beauty and truth are beautiful and true? Children have no knowledge of what I have formulated; they only feel something to that effect. As teachers we must observe this moment so we will always say the right words when needed. All of a child's later life, whether happy and secure, or alienated and paralyzed inside, depends upon what we do in this moment of crisis.

As teachers such an educational method makes it evident we must do that which will sanctify someone's entire life. If we look deeply at such a life through observation we will see how that which is brought correctly to someone during childhood will come to maturity in later life. For example, we know of people who, when they are older, perhaps already elderly, come into a group of people and they don't really have to say very much. They have a quality that brings calm, peace, and something blessed into the group. These are people who, in a wonderful way, with a moral impulse and often through the nuance of their words or the way they speak, affect others as if giving of their grace. If one is not content with the observation of life in shorter time frames, and if one makes the effort and is able to observe the whole span of an individual human life, then one knows that people who have such an effect of blessing on others had the good fortune when they were children to look up worshipfully to some others or to something that was shown to them. From this reverence, between the ages of 10 and 14, develops that which causes us to become benefactors in later life.

Expressed through imagery, what I would like to say is this: In later life, no hand can be lifted in blessing that has not learned in childhood to be folded in prayer. This is only an image to illustrate how true knowledge of human beings brings to children a living and growing feeling for the morally good and for antipathy towards evil. One has the feeling that if one were to present the sharp contours of definitions to children, it would be like putting shackles on their organism. We must give them concepts and impulses that can grow like the organism, that can grow in a soul-spiritual way and carry the inner possibility of becoming richer and richer, so that later one looks back upon the memory with happiness and the childhood life germinates in the body that has become older.

## GA 150, March 14, 1913, Page 16ff.

…In the second seven-year epoch something appears that, to a certain extent, can be understood as not happening within the continuous stream of the merely progressing Divine Beings. From a certain aspect we have already identified it many times. It appears around age 9 or 10 in the second seven-year epoch. For some, the sensitive ones, experiences occur like those I mentioned in the example of Jean Paul. With him it occurred perhaps somewhat earlier; with others it usually happens around age 9 or 10. A considerable strengthening appears, one could say an intensifying of the "I" feeling.

The fact that something special is going on can also be revealed in another way. I am not suggesting that this other way become a special educational rule, but rather if, so to speak, it should happen of itself and can be observed. One should certainly not play around with it or turn it into an educational principle. Namely: if a child around age 9 or 10 stands unclothed before a mirror, and is not already dulled by our often curious educational principles today, he or she will naturally feel a kind of fear at the sight of his or her naked body, a certain anxiety, if the child has not already been turned into a coquette by a lot of looking in the mirror.

This can be observed in children whose natural feelings are intact because they have not, up to this point, looked very much in the mirror. At this time, something evolves in human beings that acts as a kind of balance to the Luciferic stream that is there in the first epoch. In this second epoch, around the ninth or tenth year, Ahriman grasps human beings and forms, with the Ahrimanic stream, a kind of equalizing balance to the Luciferic stream. We can now bring that to completion, which is the greatest favor to Ahriman, when we, at exactly this point in time, educate the minds of growing children that are turned toward the outer world of the senses by saying to ourselves: "At this time, children must, as much as possible, be trained to be able to make their own, independent judgments."

I am mentioning an educational principle that is talked about generally in education today. Today, training to be self-reliant, directly in these years, is almost universally desired. Calculators are even provided so children do not have to properly memorize the multiplication tables. For all intents and purposes, this is based upon a certain friendliness of our era towards Ahriman.

Our era wishes, subconsciously of course, to educate children so Ahriman can be cultivated in the human soul as much as possible. And, today, when we go through the viable methods of education, as occultists, we say to ourselves: The people who represent these methods of education are only dilettantes. If Ahriman himself were to write these principles, he would be smarter about it! But these things come from real pupils of Ahriman, especially what is said about children's self-reliance and independent judgment. This, and what it indicates, will gain the upper hand more and more in the next period of time, for Ahriman will become a good controller of external powers and the ability to lead minds of our era.

**GA 194, December 6, 1919, Page 128f.**

…In lectures on education, wherever I have held them, I have also always brought attention to the fact that during the primary school years an important juncture in life occurs around age 9. One should pay very, very close attention in the primary school curriculum to this important crossroads of a human life. For instance, up to this point, one should not teach natural history in any way other than by describing natural processes through fables, legends, and the like—tied into the moral life of human beings. Then, because children are now mature enough, one should begin classic, simple, elementary descriptions of nature. Thus what one can refer to as a curriculum comes completely out of an objective, detailed observation of human beings.

I have already brought attention to this in an essay called "The Study of Man." There I indicated this time period around age 9. One can characterize this point in time: "The 'I'-consciousness gets a new form." A person will be able to look at outer nature more objectively. Earlier, everything seen in outer nature is connected with his or her own being. One's "I"-consciousness already develops in the first seven-year epoch at ages 2, 2½, and so on. But in the second phase of life, this development resumes at around age 9. This is, so to say, one of the most noticeable returns, this return of "I"-consciousness around age 9. While in the second or third year of life, the "I"-consciousness is more soul/emotional-oriented, it comes back in a more spiritual/intellectual form. That is only one of the occurrences that returns in a very conspicuous fashion. But one can see this exhibited in less significant events in a person's life as well. These intimacies of human life will be imperative for future human development, very essentially important. Insight into such things will gradually have to become a part of general education.

General human education changes from era to era. Today (isn't it true?) we are unhappy if our children get to the age of 10 and cannot yet do certain arithmetic calculations. The Romans were not quite at that point, but they were unhappy if such a youngster did not yet know the twelve times tables, while we take less care that our children learn rules and statutory provisions. The condition of our souls would also be in a bad way if that were to still take place. But that, about which one believes to be part of general consciousness, changes, and we are now standing at the beginning of an era when, out of Earth development and human development, such intimacies of soul life must become a part of general consciousness. Human beings must get to the point of more accurate self-knowledge than has been thought to be necessary up until now. Otherwise, these things will retroactively affect the condition of the whole of a human life in the worst way.

### GA 206, August 7, 1921, Page 99ff.

...In those interesting situations that play out with children from the change of teeth to puberty, we see how, to a very great degree actually, a battle is present within a becoming person. In this phase of life, to a certain degree, the etheric body, which undergoes its special organization until puberty, is fighting against the astral body. A real state of battle exists within a child. And when we contemplate the physical correlation that corresponds to this state of battle, we can say: In this phase of a child's life, there is a battle present to a pronounced degree between the growth forces and those forces that play into us through physical inspiration, through breathing. This is a very significant internal process, a process that will need to be studied more and more in order to come to know human beings. That which is mentally partially freed through the change of teeth is growth forces. Naturally, a considerable portion of these growth forces remains in the physical and secures a child's further growth. A part is freed with the change of teeth and appears as mental energy.

However, that which continues to function as growth forces fights against something that now, essentially, appears through the breathing process. That which appears through the breathing process could not appear earlier. The breathing process is certainly present, but as long as a child still has the forces involved in his or her physical growth and physical organization that come forth before the change of teeth, that which later the breathing process so noticeably and significantly affects in the human body will not take place in the organism. A large part of our developmental process is dependent upon this breathing process. Hence, by settling into the breathing process, which is achieved through the Oriental exercises that are geared specifically toward this process, one really does come into contact with something that organizes a human being through and through, something that physically brings a human being into inner flexibility which has something to do with penetrating the secrets of the world.

As has been said, before the change of teeth takes place, that which breathing actually wants with us cannot become active in the human organism. Then, however, a battle ensues of the remaining growth forces against the penetration of that which comes into a human being from out of the breathing process. The first big, significant thing that appears in relationship to the physical body as a result of the breathing process is puberty. This connection between breathing and sexual maturity has not yet been recognized by natural science. However, the connection absolutely exists. In reality, we breathe in that which sexually matures us, and also that which, in a wider sense, gives us the possibility to enter into a relationship of encompassing love with the world. We actually breathe that in.

In every natural process there is also a spiritual process. In the breathing process, there is a spiritual as well as a spiritual-soul/mental process. This spiritual-soul/mental aspect penetrates into us through the breathing process. It can enter in only when the forces have become soul/mental forces that before worked in the physical organism and have ceased their activity there with the change of teeth. Then there streams into the human being that which wants to come out of the breathing process. But those forces that have remained growth forces work against what comes out of the etheric forces, and from this comes the battle, in other words. And this battle is present between the etheric forces—between the forces that rise up from our etheric body and find their physical correlation in the metabolic system—and the astral forces in the blood circulation. Metabolism comes into the circulation (rhythmic) system.

Schematically, we can say: "We have our metabolic system which, however, enters into our blood rhythm, our blood rhythm system." The metabolic system, which is white on my diagram here, goes into the circulation system (see drawing, red). From the aspect of the etheric body, in a certain way, that is what storms upward in a human being during this period between ages 7 and 14.

The astral body works against this. We have streaming in that which rhythmically, in its physical correlation, comes from breathing, and there is a kind of fight between blood circulation rhythm (red) and breathing rhythm (blue). This is what plays out internally in a human being during this phase of life.

Speaking pictorially, with an image that may appear somewhat radical, it is approximately between the ninth and tenth years of life, with every child, when that which took place before, I would say, as a pre-encounter, a skirmish before the actual main battle, now passes over into the main battle. The astral and etheric bodies carry out their main attacks between the ninth and tenth years of life.

It is so important for teachers and educators to observe during this phase, this period of time. Teachers and educators must pay careful attention to anything and everything (it plays out differently with almost every person) that happens between the ninth and tenth years. With every child one sees something very special. Certain characteristics of temperament come to a kind of metamorphosis. Certain ideas appear. Whereas before one did well to not let children

blue
red
white

notice the difference between the "I" and the outside world, during this time period, above all, one should begin to allow the difference between the "I" and the outside world to come to the forefront. While before it was good to tell them fairy tales, wherein the processes of nature were likened to the processes of the human being in that they were personified and illustrated, now one may begin to instruct children about nature in a more formal way.

Actually, one should only teach nature stories, even in their most elementary form, beginning at this point in time. In this first stage of life, when children have begun to clearly feel the "I," at this early stage, they feel the "I" for the first time. It is a clearly defined concept; a more or less naturally clearly defined concept that joins with the "I" appears at this point in time. This is when children learn to differentiate the self from the outside world. And this corresponds to a very specific conflict between breathing rhythm and circulation rhythm, the astral body and the etheric body.

These matters always have two sides in human beings. One side presents itself in the state between waking up and going to sleep. Regarding this state, I have just explained the matter. In the state between sleeping and waking, the matter presents itself a little differently. If we have advanced to imagination and have then developed something of inspiration so that we can assess what happens through inspiration, through the breathing process, which is the physical correlation, then we find that only at this point in time, between the ninth and tenth years of life, is there a real detachment of the "I" and the astral body from the etheric and the physical bodies during sleep. For some children it will be earlier or later, but the average is between ages 9 and 10. Children, namely with the "I," are very internally connected with the physical body and etheric body, also during sleep. But from this point onward, the "I" begins to shine forth as an independent entity when the "I" and astral body do not take part in the functions of the etheric and physical bodies.

It is also true that children who die before this point—in life they go through up to the fifth, sixth, seventh, or even to the eighth or ninth years—have something that has separated them very little from the spirit-soul world which they went through between death and a new birth. These children are relatively easily pulled back into this spirit-soul world. They have, to a certain extent, only "pieced onto" a life completed with conception or birth.

When we examine these deaths, an actual cutting off of a new life is only there when children die *after* this point in time. To a certain extent, this new life does not connect in such an intensive way with the old life. Only then will the conditions be experienced that I described in my written work, *Theosophy*, in which I discuss that with children who die early, they are, in a certain way, taken back, and the life they have led on the Earth is pieced onto the life they had up to conception or birth. One can even say: A child that is present before us before this point in time between ages 9 and 10 embodies the physical-soul aspect and the spirit-soul aspect much less separately than is the case later on. A child has the spirit-soul aspect inside the physical body and that aspect works on the body. The spirit-soul aspect and the physical-soul aspect appear as a duality only after the above-mentioned time period. The later person is much more a dualistic being than is a child.

So, one must say: From this point in time, the spirit-soul aspect of a human being concerns itself less with the physical aspect than it did before. As a physical being, a child is much more of a soul-being than the later adult. During the growth period, the soul forces still thoroughly hold sway in the physical body of a child. Some soul forces still remain, though most have been transformed with the change of teeth. We can then say: In a certain way, this struggle that I have described slowly calms down after about age 12. With puberty the astral body enters into the human constitution with full authority.

However, that which detaches itself from a human being, that which later, in a certain way, is less concerned with the physical aspect, is also that which carries a person through the portal of death into the spirit-soul world when he or she dies. As has been said, in the early years of life, a child will be "thrown back" to an earlier existence; after this phase of life, a human being is separated from the previous existence, and that which detaches contains within it an embryo, in order to go through the portal of death. One can look very precisely into these things with imaginative knowledge, and one can indicate the details very clearly. One can point out how the forces that appear lead to sharply-contoured concepts but deaden the spiritual realities in whose midst we live during sleep. It is these spiritual realities that make humans into independent beings.

### GA 212, May 26, 1922, Page 126f.

… Eventually, the astral body contains an extraordinary amount because all actions are inscribed there. However, in that the "I" stands in a sympathetic relationship to everything the astral body does, the intentions and ideas out of which a person completes all of his or her actions are also inscribed. In reality, a complete integration of karma with the laws of the cosmos takes place here.

Today, with circumstances being what they are, one would like to say, with emphasis, that one knows precious little about everything that is going on internally in the human being because, namely, everything that one does not know has to do with the heart. [Translator's note: The phrase "precious little" has been translated from the German *herzlich wenig.* Steiner is making a play on words here since he is referring to the human heart, and the German word for heart is *Herz.*] One knows what happens here in the physical world and observes it according to natural laws. One knows what people do morally and observes it according to moral laws. But all that happens morally in a human life on the one hand, and all that happens physically on the other, is merged within the human heart so that one finds these two things that today function side by side so independently in human beings—moral events and physical events merged together in the human heart, if one really learns to understand the configuration of the human heart in its totality. That means, what happens in this heart happens in a naturally, much more concealed fashion than openly takes place with the change of teeth. We inherit teeth and we then form teeth out of our organism. The first ones fall out, and the others stay with us. The first teeth have a certain tendency to succumb. If they did not fall out, they would still not be able to endure. The remaining teeth are ruined primarily by outside things, including, naturally, outer things in the organism itself.

With puberty, in an invisible way, our first etheric heart surrenders to decay and we gain a kind of permanent heart, a kind of ether heart. This remaining ether heart is the first that is completely suited to fully take up our activity. Therefore, it is indeed something completely different if a person dies before or after reaching puberty. If a person dies before reaching puberty, there is only a tendency for that which was done on the Earth to be passed on through karma. Single things can be incorporated into karma even if a child dies before reaching puberty, but there is always something vague and enigmatic about it. Proper formation of karma happens only from the moment the astral heart fully launches into the etheric heart, where they connect. But, it is also, if I may express it like this, the organism of karma formation. With death, what is concentrated in the human being and has merged together will become more and more cosmic and later will be incorporated into the person from out of the cosmos in the next earthly life.

Everything that we do is not just our concern alone. It is true that something is incorporated in us that comes out of the cosmos and also maintains the tendency to surrender our acts to the cosmos. Karmic laws effectively prove and crystallize these acts in order to form our karma so that what the cosmos makes out of our acts, by its effect, will be carried into life again at the beginning of the next earthly life.

## GA 217, October 12, 1922, Page 153

What I am saying should not be used to create another intellectual theory about education, but rather there should be an artistic atmosphere created between young and old. Only when this happens will there appear what is needed so today's young people can grow into the world in a healthy way. What they grow into can be described very precisely: Between ages 9 and 10 there lives in the soul of every person who is not a psychopath a vague feeling. There needs be no clear, or even unclear, definition present, but it begins to live in a person beginning around age 9 or 10. Up to that time a person's soul life was only concerned with what is called the astral body. From that time on, the person's "I"-force becomes active. This stirring of the "I"-force in the human being does not live in formulated definitions, but in perception. In the deep unconscious of the soul, a question settles into the mind of a growing person. It is one thing with one person and something else with another.

Summarized in a concept it would perhaps go something like this: Until now the astral body believed in other people, but now I need to have whatever one says to me be such that I can believe in him or others in my environment. Those who, as children, rebel against something like this are those who need it the most. Between ages 9 and 10 one begins to depend upon believing in an older person in order to fortify the "I." One must be able to believe in someone without having it drummed in. One must be able to believe in a person through the artistic atmosphere that has been created.

And woe if nothing happens from the side of the elder person to answer this question in the right way that some children keep with them up to age 16 or 17, and some even to age 18 or 19. The young person should be able to say: "I am grateful that I have been able to learn from my elder what can be learned only from him. What he can say to me, only he can say. If I learn this when I am older, it would already be different."

## GA 232, November 25, 1923, Page 47f.

We are not beings who merely stand at the door of nature and knock in vain. Through that which is in our innermost self we stand in the closest relationship to the intrinsic being of nature. However, because up to age 7 children have a physical body that is completely inherited, nothing from the "I," from its gesture and physiognomy, goes over into the inner being of nature. Beginning with the change of teeth, we start to penetrate the inner essence of nature. Only after the change of teeth have we matured enough to gradually begin to reflect and ponder on anything in nature. Before this time, what rises up in children is only capricious and arbitrary thoughts, which have little to do with nature. They are appealing precisely because they have very little to do with nature. We approach children in the best way when we are poetic in their presence—when the stars are the eyes of the sky, and so forth, when the things we speak of are removed as far as possible from external physical reality.

Beginning with the change of teeth onward, children gradually grow into nature so that their thoughts can little by little coincide and concur with the thoughts of nature. And basically, from ages 7 to 14, the whole life of a child is one of growing into nature, because, besides his or her soul memories, a child also carries his or her unique gesture and physiognomy into nature. And it continues like that throughout one's whole life. As far as intrinsic nature is concerned, with the change of teeth we are born as a singular, human individuality.

## GA 297, September 24, 1919, Page 108

Starting in the ninth year of life, there begins to be the possibility of developing "I"-perception in such a way that, for example, children can be approached with events in nature stories and natural descriptions of the world of plants and animals.

## GA 297, November 27, 1919, Page 172f.

When a person has reached approximately the ninth year of life, a new phase begins. It is not as clearly delineated as it is around age 7, but it still has a certain kind of clarity. The aftereffects of the impulse to imitate gradually disappear and something appears for a child that, although intimate, can be observed if one wishes to see it. There appears a special relationship of the child to his or her own "I." The relationship to the "I," which one could call a soul relationship, naturally appears much earlier. It appears at the very moment that, looking back on one's life, one can first remember. This is also approximately the time when a child transitions from saying: "Carl wants that" or "Marie wants that" to "I want that." Later, one can remember back to this point in time. What has happened earlier is usually completely forgotten by most people. The "I" mentally enters into the internal human being. But it is not yet completely there intellectually. This, which actually appears intellectually in the mental-soul constitution of a human being as the experience of the "I," indicates what is happening with a child between ages 9 and 10, approximately.

Other people who have been observers of the soul have sometimes alluded to this great and significant moment in a human life. Jean Paul told so beautifully how, as a very young boy, he could clearly remember standing in front of a barn at his parents' farm—he said it so articulately—and the "I"-consciousness awakened in him. He said he would never forget it, how he peered into the most destiny-laden sanctity of the human soul.

For some it is distinct, for others less so, but around age 9 such a change occurs. This point in time is extraordinarily important for education. If we are successful in stimulating the feelings and cultivating the directions of the will in growing children that one refers to as religious or moral, and which one can summon from all the other subjects taught, then one need only be a good observer of children. When one sees this phase approaching, when one can observe it, the authority of a teacher will have the effect of anchoring precisely those religious feelings that were sparked earlier in preparation for this stage.

At this point in time it is decided whether a person, from his or her deepest inner regions, can look up in honesty and truth to something that divinely, thoroughly ensouls and imbues the world and human lives with spirit. And those who can see into a human life through spiritual vision will, one wants to say, be intuitively led, at precisely this point in time, to find the right words and the right rules of conduct as a teacher.

What education is, in truth, is something artistic. One must not approach children with education as a standardized science, but with education as an art. Just as an artist must master his or her material, must know it intimately and in detail, so someone who is permeated with spiritual vision will know the symptoms that rise up around age 9, when a person is so internally immersed that his or her "I"-consciousness becomes a spirit consciousness, whereas before it was a soul consciousness. Then, educators who had previously always relied upon those things that tied into human subjectivity will transition to a more objective observation of things.

One will know, if one understands how to confront this at the right time, that before this point in time one should only speak to children about natural science, observation of nature for example, so that these things are clothed in stories, fables, and parables. Everything in the way of observations of nature and natural objects should be compared to human characteristics. In short, they should be handled in such a way that human beings are not separated from the natural environment. At the moment around age 9 when the "I" awakens, a human being separates from the natural environment of his or her own accord. A person will now be mature enough to make objective comparisons between natural phenomena. Therefore, before this point in time in childhood, we should not begin with objective descriptions of the natural world that surrounds human beings. We should much more develop an accurate sense, I would like to say a spiritual instinct, for this momentous change.

**Page 179f.**

One must realize how two human mental-soul faculties are connected. Today's psychology, which in reality is not penetrated by spiritual science, finds no connection between these faculties. When we are able to correctly regard the important point in time that I have described as being around age 9, we will see that at this time something special is going on in relation to the feeling faculties, the emotional life of children. Human beings internalize things and other nuances of feeling appear. In a certain way, the inner soul life, in its nuances of feeling, becomes more independent from external nature. In contrast, something also appears that comes to meet us only through really intimate observation of the soul. Jean-Paul noticed this also and expressed it ingeniously: We certainly learn more in our first three years of life than in our first three years of academic life because, in a manner of speaking, we still have an organically developed memory, because, at that time, the memory still functions organically. That is to say, for our life, we learn more at that time. However, around age 9, a special relationship that plays more into conscious life is created between the life of feelings/emotions and the life of memory.

One must only be aware of such things. If they cannot be seen, they are as if not there. If one really penetrates and cultivates this intimate relationship between feeling-life and memory, one discovers the correct way of looking at it and how to appeal to the memory during school lessons. One really should not call upon memory without calling upon the life of feeling at the same time. That is to say, for lessons involving stories, one will find the right nuance of communication if one realizes: That which should be incorporated into the memory should, through our presentation, always be steeped in something that plays over into a perception sense that has become more independent. One will also put the story lessons in the proper place in the lesson plan if one knows about how these things are connected. In this way, one will also gain the correct outlook about memory culture in general. And, with that through which one has particularly acted upon the memory, one will also act upon the feeling-life just as previously the will-life was acted upon through artistic endeavors.

After this phase of life, one will gradually gain the possibility of letting the intellectual element work from out of the elements of will and feeling. With education, if it happens that the intellectual element is not formed in the correct way out of the elements of will and feeling, we are working against the developmental forces in a human being, without keeping those forces in mind.

### GA 297, May 21, 1920, Page 193

The ninth year becomes ( … ) a Rubicon. In their inner consciousness, children detach and differentiate from the environment. They make the distinction between self and surroundings, but they will remain lovingly devoted to their surroundings.

### Page 194

During the years between the change of teeth and puberty one should not count on a child's faculty of reasoning, but rather teach every concept figuratively, pictorially. For example, if one wishes to present the idea of the immortality of the human soul so that the concept is understood, one can offer the images of the development of a butterfly. However, it is essential that teachers also believe that whatever imagery is used is representative of the concept.

At age 9 children begin to segregate from the environment. Now we can begin to appeal to their independent reasoning powers.

Spiritual science draws the curriculum from the observed development of children. It takes the world as it really is and, for this reason, is something eminently practical.

**GA 297a, February 24, 1924, Page 26f.**

Further, we observe that between ages 9 and 10, up to age 11, there is an important turning point for children. Those who can observe life in the appropriate way know that between ages 9 and 11 lies a point of development that, depending on how it is recognized by teachers and educators, can influence children's internal, and often external, destinies either favorably or unfavorably. Up to this point in time, children detach very little from the environment. Before age 9 one must take care they receive a different description of a plant than after age 9. Before that time children identify with everything in the surroundings; then they learn to differentiate from the environment; and then they first meet the concept of "I." Before that, children have only an "I"-perception. We must observe how children behave, for example how, from this point in time onward they begin to formulate questions differently. We must respond to each and every individual at this important time because it is crucial to everything that follows for the rest of his or her life.

For instance, we must be clear in our minds as to such things as physics and the like, which are completely disassociated from human beings, that they can accomplish a kind of perfection only when everything that is subjective is excluded from the formulation of their laws, and that these subjects may be presented to children beginning only at age 11 or 12. In contrast, we begin teaching the customary foreign languages in a practical way already at the beginning of primary school. One sees that, in reality, through the fact that we do not teach foreign languages using a translation process, but rather by enabling children to get into the spirit of another language, their entire soul structure is broadened.

**GA 297a, February 28, 1921, Page 56ff.**

One must realize, if one wishes to teach in the correct way, that between ages 9 and 10½ is an extraordinarily important time in child development. It is the time when children are so deeply immersed internally that they learn to differentiate their own self from nature and the rest of their environment. Before this point in time, which is a strong turning point in a human life, children basically see their surroundings in pictures because they are still interwoven with their own inner life, in pictures, which are often symbolic in nature. A child thinks about his or her surroundings in a symbolic way. Later, another epoch occurs: Children differentiate their own self from nature and the external environment.

It is enormously significant at this time in life (for one child a little later, for another a little earlier) that teachers are able to assess it in the correct way. The way teachers behave correctly with children between ages 9 and 10—fatherly/motherly, friendly, lovingly guiding them over this Rubicon—greatly impacts human lives for the rest of their existence, remaining until physical death. Whether someone can have a vibrant, fresh attitude about life during critical moments, or carry a dreariness of soul throughout his or her life, depends in many regards (although not all) upon how teachers behave with a child between ages 9 and 10½. Sometimes it simply has to do with finding the right word at the right moment, perhaps when a boy or girl meets a teacher in the hallway and asks something that the right countenance is found in which to answer. The art of education is not something that can be learned or taught abstractly, any more than painting or sculpting or any other art. It is something that is based upon endless particulars arising from a tactfulness of soul. This tactfulness of soul can be attained through anthroposophical spiritual science.

One must also distinguish between what one brings to children before this important time between ages 9 and 10½ and what one brings after. Above all, one must take into consideration that in our current, advanced civilization we have something that has become external, abstract, and emblematic. If you look back to ancient civilizations and any pictography, you will see it was still focused on that which accommodated the meaning. It was turned into a picture to which the human being was linked, and wherewith the human being, through perception and feelings, lived. Today everything has become symbols. We may not teach reading and writing as if it is something foreign because before age 9 children are joined with—identify with—the surroundings. We may not teach out of the abstract, as it is done today.

In the Waldorf school we introduce children to learning in a thoroughly artistic way by first allowing the drawing of forms, even colorful form drawing, and painting that unfolds out of the fullness of humanity. We let the children do this first, and then, when we lead them further in this manner of drawing/painting, we develop the letters of the alphabet from this drawing of forms, which become writing.

## Page 58f.

Those who wish always to have clarity and more clarity that is adapted to a child's understanding do not realize what it means for a person's entire life if they, let us say, at age 8 or 9 or from 10–15 years old have accepted something on the authority of a teacher; if a respected authority figure tells one something and it is held to be true because he or she said it. It still lies over the horizon, but one takes it into one's soul. Perhaps one will not recall it again until age 35 or 40. What one has already received memory-wise is now, with the strength of maturity, understood. This consciousness related to awareness of having become mature, of being able to pull something up from memory, refreshes and quickens the soul forces in a way that is not highly valued in ordinary life. If one wishes to tailor everything to a child's ability to understand at age 8, 9, or 12, the soul is made desolate. This is something that must be said today because, out of their materialistic clever understanding, people are no longer in a position to see what is natural, right and essential in such areas.

Out of the substrata of human nature, out of that which wants to form and develop from week to week and year to year, the curriculum for such a school will be obtained, as it is in Waldorf schools. Such a curriculum unfolds entirely out of the knowledge about the human being. It is no abstract curriculum. It is rather something that is an underlying basis for education in these schools just like painting skills are for a painter and sculpting skills are for someone who wishes to work as a sculptor.

**GA 297a, November 4, 1922, Page 153ff.**

When a child stands in the primary school years between ages 9 and 10, a teacher with real understanding perhaps faces his or her greatest challenge. At that time teachers will notice most of the children they have been entrusted with will approach them and seem to need something especially. Children will not always speak up. In fact more often than not the questions they have remain unspoken and live merely in the realm of feelings and perceptions. These questions can take on hundreds or even thousands of forms. It depends very little upon giving a child a particular answer. If one prefers one answer or another, the content makes little difference. However, what makes a big difference is that one elicits the right feeling of trust in a child with the right countenance of soul, that one meets a child with the right sense of feeling at exactly the right moment for what always appears between ages 9 and 10.

I could characterize this moment in a variety of ways. When we teach children we notice that before this moment, which occurs sometime between ages 9 and 10, they cannot rightly differentiate from the environment or rightly experience their "I," even though they have long referred to themselves as "I." In this moment of life children learn to rightly differentiate from the environment. We can now no longer affect them with mere fairytales or all kinds of lessons in which the external world is enlivened. Now we can begin to turn our attention to things that prompt them to differentiate their "I" from the external world.

Something else that is essentially different appears that is very deeply connected with developing morality. In the beginning of the epoch in which children are devoted to authority, they accept an authority figure as they are. Between ages 9 and 10, children feel, in a certain way, forced to look past an authority figure to that which actually carries that person. This does not have to be on a conscious level. It can be deep in the feeling-nature, in the subconscious, as one says, but it is there. An authority figure says: "That is true, that is good, and that is beautiful."

But now children want to feel and perceive from where an authority figure is getting all this. What is this knowledge about the good, true, and beautiful? What is in the desire for truth, goodness, and beauty? This comes about because that which is kept in what I would describe as the substrata of the soul, which at the beginning of childhood is a piously-sense-related, giving-oneself-up-to the external world, if I may be allowed the use of such a curious expression, disappears from the soul's underground and rises up as if from the deepest regions of the soul. That which was sense-related in infants up to the change of teeth, the material sense perceptions that are the embryo of all later religious feelings vis-à-vis the world, emerges in the soul between ages 9 and 10 and becomes a need of the soul.

One must know this and anticipate it, just as one lovingly cares for a seed so it grows into a plant. That which was once within a child, and prepared itself like an embryonic seed through the material senses, is now before one as an element of soul, and one must care for it with that in mind. In this way one plants a religious seed. This creates a special relationship with a child.

Later on, around age 17 up to age 18 teachers will notice that which came to light in a soul-feeling way as religious feeling now appears in a spiritual way and is poured out into the will so a person forms his or her religious conceptions during this time.

It is extraordinarily important to penetrate the basis of these things if one wishes to teach in a meaningful way in accordance with truth and reality. Nature has already provided for the physical organism, otherwise one could not be certain, especially if it happened to come from a modern, futuristic painter, that people would not get the idea to put an ear in the wrong place, or some such thing. Such things could happen...

### Page 155ff.

We must not try to nourish religious feelings in children in any form other than as soul preparation before the described time between ages 9 and 10. In regard to children, we must have this period of time well in hand. What you brought earlier in the way of religious feelings and concepts remained outside of a child. The child accepted those things on your authority. However, between ages 9 and 10, something awakens in a child. If you discern this, you will direct those feelings, which seemingly want to come out of the soul of their own accord, into a religious sense. Then you will have helped a child become a religiously true human being. Today, there is so little actual genuine psychology for our time. Otherwise, people would know where the incorrect religious feelings and perceptions that are so prevalent in social life today originate. It is believed to be possible to develop anything in a human being at any age because one does not know what must be brought out of the soul of a child precisely between ages 9 and 10.

### GA 301, April 26, 1920, Page 83

We must be clear about this: The fact that we divide the primary school years into three epochs is what provides us with a basis for determining our lesson plans and educational goals. Beginning primary school years: Authority principle is woven into imitation. Ages 9–12: Authority principle encroaches more and more; mere imitation recedes. Children begin to separate their "I" from the surroundings.

Age 12: Reasoning faculties awaken. This "I" calls upon children to use their own powers of judgment.

**Page 86**

If one has acquired a real talent for observation, one can also discern things even with a large class. One can see that when one brings an artistic element to children (which is only later abstracted and intellectualized) in the way I have sketched it out for you, their physiognomy changes. Truly, small variations appear in bodily physiognomy, and between ages 7 and 9 children are so internally engaged there appears something healthily active, not nervously active, in children's facial physiognomy. It is eminently important to a person's whole life that this happens because, through the appearance of this healthily active moment in the physiognomy, one also develops later in life love for the world, feeling for the world, and inner healing forces against all kinds of hypochondria, superfluous criticism, and the like. Actually, as a teacher it is really terrible if this is not achieved at around age 9 and the children are not, even externally, purely in their physiognomy, something different than they were before.

**GA 303, December 31, 1921, Page 158ff.**

This becomes different with the change of teeth. Certain forces become more soul-spiritual in nature, and they now come into action only through the movements that are expressed in the heart, in the breathing rhythm. They no longer work in the material processes to the same degree. In contrast, they are now in the respiratory and circulation system, separated from the physical. One can also physically observe this in that the breathing rhythm, the circulation pulse, becomes stronger at this age. At this age children have an inner impulse and drive to experience that which gradually becomes the independent soul-spiritual aspect, as rhythm and timing, rhythm and pulse, that first takes place in their own bodies.

Of course, this inner drive is instinctual and not on a conscious level. Children have a longing for this playback of rhythm and pulse in their own organization. It is important to bear in mind that everything that is brought before a child after the change of teeth should be designed in such a way that the rhythm of it will allow for its integration in the way he or she actually wants it. As a teacher and an educational artist, one must, in a certain way, be able to live in a rhythmic element so that a child responds and feels as if he or she is in his or her own element.

Something else also begins with this. If breathing and circulation rhythm is not handled in the right way at this age, in a certain way it is ruined for the whole of later life. Many weaknesses and conditions of disease located in the organs of breathing and circulation have their origins in the wrong kind of education during the school years. Also at this phase, through different effects of the etheric (or formative forces) body, children form in such a way that the limbs are greatly lengthened at this time. The life of the muscles and bones, of the skeleton, plays a special role at the change of teeth and wants to conform to the life of breathing and circulation.

During this phase children grow in such a way that the muscles vibrate in synchrony with the breathing and circulation rhythm; a child's whole being wants to adopt a musical nature. While before children were plastically active in their own bodies, now they begin to become musicians, unconscious musicians that work into their bodies according to an inner impulse. And that is the essential thing with children that one recovers in school, that one knows one is dealing with an unconscious musician within a child. One must meet this inner impulse so that a child wishes to treat his or her own organization so that it behaves as a new violin being played, so that a child finds the way with his or her own organization into the hills and valleys of the waves. Only with human beings, of course, all of this is growth. At the very most, a violin can be ruined only once, but human beings can be made to absorb false growth principles which then grow continually larger and stronger and have a ruinous effect on the rest of their lives.

Once one has taken the path of knowledge of the human being that is effective for education and didactics, one will find that this general nature, which I have now specifically characterized, is pervasive throughout the primary school years from the change of teeth up to puberty. However, in turn, this life phase falls into three periods that can be clearly defined. The first lasts from the change of teeth to approximately completion of the ninth year, the second up to about the twelfth year, and the third from about age 13 up to sexual maturity.

One can get insights into how these three periods in childhood are different precisely from that which children experience internally as musical. In the first period, up to about the end of age 9, children want to live out everything that comes near and penetrates in an inner rhythm, an inner rhythmic pulse, so they connect with the breathing and heart rhythm. Through this they are indirectly joined with that which determines how the muscles and bones form. And if this merging does not take place, if the one does not, in a certain way, go over into the other, a person develops, though not immediately visible externally, as a kind of internal cripple.

Up to the end of age 9, children definitely have the aspiration to internally live out everything rhythmically. With a perceptive eye, one is able to respond to children's inner soul organization; one can absolutely recognize that when children of this age hear music, they actually translate everything musical into an internal rhythm. Children vibrate along. They form internally according to that which is perceived externally.

That is to say, at this age children are still something of what they were before. Before and up to the time of the change of teeth, children were, to a large extent, sense-organs—not a sense-organ that functions in a conscious way, but one that, ultimately, like the other sense-organs, unconsciously reproduces the external world. As I have explained, up to the time of the change of teeth, children are absolute imitators. If you consider the human eye, and refrain from that which is taken into the life of imagination through the eye, in the true sense and meaning of the eye organization, something manifests itself within the eye so the environment will be internally reproduced.

These emulations, or reproduced images, first take possession of the life of imagination. There the life of imagination attaches itself to the life of the senses. Very young children are completely, unconsciously sense-organs. That is to say, very young children internally reproduce what they perceive from people in the environment. However, these inner images are not simply pictures but are, at the same time, forces that materially, plastically, internally organize.

When the time of the change of teeth arrives, these emulations, or reproduced images, go only into the system of movement, the rhythmic system; that is the only place they want to go. Certainly, something still remains behind as a plastic, malleable formation, but the other aspect that was not there before to the same extent now appears with it. There is a difference between the way children behave toward rhythm and rhythmic beat before the change of teeth and after. Before the change of teeth, rhythm and rhythmic beat are things children certainly imitate, but they are changed into an element of plasticity. Later, they are changed into an internal musical element.

When children have reached the end of the ninth year and up to the twelfth year, they begin to gain an understanding of rhythm, beat, and melody in and of itself. Children no longer desire as much to reproduce the rhythmic element internally. They perceive it as such, as a structure that stands outside of their own self. Before, rhythm and beat were experienced, but after, children begin to develop understanding and comprehension. This state of developing understanding lasts until around age 12, not only for all that is musical, but also for everything that comes to meet them from the world. Around age 12, or perhaps a little earlier, children begin to have the ability to transfer their desire to experience everything musical and rhythmic in a way that is subject to imagination over to a desire to experience those things subject to thinking.

For everything that is looked at with spiritual eyes, with that acute gaze, one can also see the outer bodily-physical cooperation that occurs. I have said before that a child wishes to pattern his or her muscle and bone formation after what is there in the inner being. Now, towards age 12, a child begins to wish to live not merely in rhythm, but rather to let the feeling of rhythm and rhythmic pulse flow out into the abstract-thinking element. So during this time, the part of the muscle that is phased into pure tendon is gradually concentrated and strengthened. Before this time all movement is more aligned with the muscle as such, but afterward it is directed more to that which has flowed out into pure tendon. Everything that transpires in the soul-spiritual aspect one finds again in the bodily-physical aspect. And this incorporation of the life of the tendon, the connection of bone and muscle, is the outer physical expression of the purely feeling-oriented, rhythmic element sailing into that which is now the logical element, that which no longer has rhythm and beat. What one has gained in knowledge of human beings must absolutely be taken into consideration in the art of education.

### GA 303, January 2, 1922, Page 204

If we observe children using true, objective knowledge of human beings, it becomes apparent that, from the point in time between ages 9 and 10 up to about the end of age 10, everything children mentally process is done in such a way that primarily the muscle system is working everywhere in cooperation with growth forces. At this time there is nothing else going on within a child other than the muscle system's working in cooperation with the mental-soul aspect, namely within the more intimate growth forces. Inner swelling and lengthening of the muscles is essentially dependent upon how the soul forces develop. Typical in the childhood years between ages 9 and 10 is that the muscles have an intimate relationship to the respiratory and circulatory system. The muscle system inclines toward the respiratory and circulatory system. This is what we are appealing to with a truly artful method of education. That is, we influence the muscle system circuitously by way of the respiratory and circulatory system.

Toward age 12 something completely different appears. The muscles turn away from their intimate relationship with the respiratory and circulatory system and turn toward the skeletal system, the bones, in such a way that from that time forward the muscles conform and adapt to the skeleton. While before this time growth principles in the muscles conformed to breathing and blood circulation, they now adapt to the dynamics of the skeletal system. Using growth forces, the muscles participate in everything that we transact through the skeletal system, actually, the limb system—walking, grasping, and jumping. Muscles turn away from a direct communication with the respiratory and circulatory system and create an intimacy with the skeletal system.

In this way the whole human being adapts to the outside world in a very powerful way and in a still more powerful way from the age of 12 onward than was previously the case. Before this time a person is directed inward by his or her muscle system. The muscles would grow as they could within an internally enclosed rhythmic system. Movement was an appeal to the muscle system and bone formation was merely hauled along, so to speak. Toward age 12, it is completely different. Through muscle growth, a human being becomes positioned within the mechanics and dynamics of the skeletal system.

**Page 205**

Notice how a human being actually adapts to the world: With a very young child the plastically formative forces reside in the brain and radiate out from there. Those forces then go over to the muscles. When children have reached age 12, they put their entire being into the skeletal system and then go out into the world; only then do they go out. Human beings go thoroughly through themselves before coming to a relationship with the whole world. First we have the head forces, which are later poured into the muscles and then into the bones.

## GA 303, January 5, 1922, Page 351ff.

*Dr. Steiner:* The choleric temperament essentially comes about because at any of the particular points in life occurring around age 2 and then again at the time I have indicated between ages 9 and 10, the ego ("I") is having an especially strong effect. There are other similar periods of time, but we are mainly dealing with the first two. The "I" is not something that simply appears at the age of 21. It is only released at a certain age but it is, of course, always present in human beings. From birth, or rather, beginning three weeks after conception, the ego is present. It can happen that the ego becomes overly intense. Then it has an especially strong effect at these particular points of time. Just observe what in actual fact is the reason for these special points of time in life.

Between ages 9 and 10 we have a quite special working of the "I" to the effect that human beings learn to differentiate from the environment. For a condition of normalcy to exist, it is necessary to have a special state of equilibrium. This special state of balance can be shifted to the outside. In that case it is also one of the many causes of a sanguine temperament. I have stated explicitly, since I was dealing with this matter yesterday, there are various factors working together. Yesterday I discussed specifically those factors that come into question with a particular viewpoint in mind.

It is also possible at this time for the point of balance in accordance with the inner aspect to be lost. It may happen when a child learns to speak, or even when he or she learns to maintain a vertical position by standing upright. There is opportunity everywhere for the "I" to work too strongly. One must be attentive to this and try not to do anything wrong at these points in time. One has already done something wrong if, for example, one forces a child to stand upright too soon. It should absolutely take place as something imitative. A child should stand upright only when the capacity is there to imitate the upright position of adults.

Perhaps one will come to an especially clear understanding if one considers what something like the upright position actually means for the human being. Essentially, accounting for exceptions, of course (but exceptions also can be explained by their exceptional nature), animals are constituted so their spinal columns lie parallel to the Earth's surface. Human beings are constituted so the normal position of the spinal column is the same as the direction of the Earth's radius. This is the radical difference between human beings and animals. Within this radical difference between humankind and animals lies that which one simply has to respond to when the purely Darwinian materialists (I do not say Darwinians, but rather Darwinian materialists) argue that an essential difference between a human skeleton and an animal skeleton is not present since both have the same number of bones, etc. Fine. That is true, but animal skeletons have horizontal spines and human beings' spines are vertical. A relationship to the whole cosmos is expressed in the vertical position of the spine. This relationship means that a human being will actually become the bearer of an ego. Animals have a threefold nature: physical body, etheric body (or body of formative forces), and astral body. An ego is possible only if a being is organized vertically.

I have spoken of this once before in a lecture. Afterward, someone came to me and said: "Yes, but how is it when a person sleeps and the spine is horizontal?" Such things are absolutely not understood in the way they were intended. Naturally, there is more to it than the fact that human beings have spines constructed to be vertical and are in fact vertical when they stand upright. It also has to do with the whole structure of the human being. It has to do with the fact that all the ratios and corresponding positions of the bones are together in such a way that, in conditions of full growth, while walking, human beings have a vertical spine, while that of animals is horizontal. That is to say, it really has to do with the fact that in this verticalness of the spine, the indicator is present which points to the human being as the bearer of an ego.

**GA 304, February 27, 1921, Page 228f.**

At around age 9 (it can last up to age 10 or even 11) is an extraordinarily important phase in children's development. As teachers and educators we go through this period with the children as their leaders and guides. In the first years of life, children learn language. They gradually learn to refer to their own selves as "I." However, up until approximately age 9, this differentiation of one's own "I" from the environment is still somewhat undefined. Those with the power of accurate observation know that children cross a Rubicon at this time. Between ages 9 and 11 children learn to differentiate their own selves from the environment. For some children it happens a little earlier and for some a little later, but always sometime within the described period of time. One senses or feels that a child is completing the process of differentiating the self from external nature. A child no longer feels as if he or she were a conscious appendage of a larger organism, but rather like an independent being.

How one behaves in the presence of children during this time period has an enormous influence on the rest of their lives. The correct approach at this time will produce a lasting well of joy and enthusiasm for life in a child. In contrast, if one does not approach a child in the right way, sullenness and a dreary, dull attitude toward life is cultivated. Keep in mind that up to this point in time, one approaches children through pictures to which their own nature can relate. Since a child's nature is not yet able to differentiate the self from the environment, one must keep in mind that everything is understood through imagery, a connection of the human being with the environment should be shown.

## GA 304, September 26, 1921, Page 78ff.

One can quite accurately see in a child's organism when he or she goes through the change of teeth—the physical-soul element is separated out. The physical body becomes one-sided and hardened. One sees how actually the same forces which function within normal limits in the higher spheres function within the processes of illness if they become overgrown. Within normal processes, that which leads into illness, if it becomes overgrown, is always present. We can say that human beings are on the tip of illness when they get teeth. The more we engage that which now wants to be released as something soul-spiritual (in anthroposophical terminology we call it the etheric body) in such a way that is completely suited to the physical-bodily aspect of a child so that we quasi replicate the physical-bodily aspect in this soul-spiritual aspect, the more healthy an effect we will have on a child. We must learn about this physical body that is prone to sickness and health because we must cultivate it into that which comes out of a child as a soul-spiritual aspect (etheric body).

Let us take a look at the other end of the primary school years—puberty. We have the exact opposite process. During the change of teeth, something extracts itself from a child's organism during which the physical body, to a certain extent, is repelled from the soul-spiritual aspect, which is then released in sexual maturity. We have the henceforth developed soul-spiritual aspect, which in turn wants to return to the physical body. It permeates and saturates the physical body.

Conversely, in sexual maturity we have a submersion of the soul-spiritual aspect into the physical aspect. The physical body is soaked in the mushrooming, instinctively-functioning, soul-spiritual aspect. This is the reverse process. This is the process that follows the opposing side of becoming ill. This process tends to pursue, I want to say, an inner sense of well-being and feelings of being imbued with happiness. This is the opposite pole. Insofar as we educate children in the primary school years we must really have this condition of balance well in hand continuously—the balance between that which gravitates toward the soul-spiritual element from the change of teeth onward in order to be released and that which gravitates from the soul-spiritual element back into the physical body. We must try to always maintain the balance between this back and forth which is present the entire time during the primary school years.

This becomes an especially important and fascinating task between ages 9 and 10, where, as a result of such conflicting forces, children are in such a state that they are literally leaning in all possible directions. It depends solely upon a teacher whether he or she is perhaps a good counselor for a child at the right moment between ages 9 and 10, that the right words are spoken, or perhaps withheld, and so on. It matters immensely for someone's whole life that a teacher understands how to correctly interact with children between ages 9 and 10. But, you see, only when one correctly understands this interweaving action of the soul-spiritual and physical-bodily aspects can one understand what a child really is and what is within a child that needs to be addressed.

It is absolutely not possible to even discuss education and didactics without considering these ascending and descending processes, which are only one-sided if they are referred to separately as soul-spiritual or bodily-physical aspects. These processes are always both of those things flowing into each other. Flowing into each other is the reality. Children can be understood only if one understands how to form into a whole that which has been identified as two separate aspects and how they work together.

What is one to do with the child from the time of the change of teeth forward? One has to do such that one continually sees to it that the part of the soul-spiritual element that wishes to be released really forms itself to suit the purposes of growth in a human being. In a certain way we have to recreate that which wants to come out of the organism, also in the soul-spiritual aspect. We have to know a person and provide him or her with that which brings the entire harmony of his or her being into activity. We have to draw out everything from a person's inner being.

As a child draws closer to the time of sexual maturity, we have to look for that which a person is in the fact that he or she allows the soul-spiritual aspect to submerge into the physical body. A person will develop abnormally and become an internally agitated person, a nervous or neurasthenic person (I will not even describe the other possible conditions) if, at this age, we do not realize how we should permeate and infuse that which submerges into the physical-bodily organization with interests for the outside world.

We must guide a person in such a way that he or she becomes interested in the outside world and that which connects someone to the outside world is taken into the physical organization as much as possible. We must understand what wants to come out of a child when he or she is entrusted to us for primary schooling in order that we may recreate it for the child. We must have knowledge of the world in order to know in what a person could become interested if we wish to provide that person's submerging soul-spiritual aspect with something he or she will not allow to sink into carnality and descend into lasciviousness. Through interests in the world, we help a person become someone who lives with the world and gets away from the ego-self, someone who does not expand into egoism, does not glow with egoism, but rather has a right and harmonious relationship with the world.

These are the things that can show you how an effective, well-thought out method of education and didactics that is based on the whole human being must be approached. Naturally, I can only indicate these things to you. As I have experienced again recently, it is painful when one speaks often of such things to today's teachers and educators and they say to you: "Yes, that is strange; there exists coincidentally a lot of medical knowledge in what you say!" Naturally, the medical insights are not there "coincidentally," but rather they belong quite necessarily in a system of education. Without them, a healthy educational system is unthinkable. It would lose itself in abstractions that are empty of content and would be of no use in dealing with children.

### GA 304a, March 26, 1923, Page 44ff.

Education in morality and ethics during primary school years is accomplished only through the presentation/description of the intrinsic essence of the concept, with which one makes clear, vivid and concrete that which is felt, perceived moral judgment. It depends on this whether children at this age, by the clearly conveyed view of the concept of morality, develop sympathy for the moral and ethical and antipathy for the immoral and unethical. It does not depend upon whether one gives them a rule or precept; those do not penetrate into the soul. That which is fixed in a child's soul as perceived moral judgment, by way of sympathies and antipathies, determines his or her entire inner culture of morality.

And just how important it is to have a right, moral relationship with children is especially supported by one single fact. If one can teach from a real, inwardly practical psychology (up to a specific point in time around age 9 or 10—it varies with individuals), also in respect to children's moral judgments, sympathies, and antipathies that one can cultivate in them, one will notice they live more in the world. In spite of the fact that children still have what I would describe as "biological egoism," they can forget themselves, feel connected with the world, and still merge into it.

Let us say, for example, the requirements for having accurate insight into the developmental phase of children between ages 9 and 10 for object lessons are also particularly needed for education in morals and ethics. Between ages 9 and 10 a curious thing emerges within a developing human being. There is this curious fact that, especially at this time, children need one to be very observant of individuals and what comes out of different children.

Sometimes at this point in time, a child will say something from which one will sense the need to find a few words that will help him or her further along. In these snatches of time, a child crosses a life moment in which everything can depend upon whether he or she is met with the right words and the right behavior. What is this life moment? It is the moment when, through the struggle with languages after a child's whole inner life falls together and is in concurrence with languages, he or she becomes very consciously aware: There is a difference between me and the world.

In the first few years of life children learn to say "I" completely unconsciously. But now they acutely demand orientation of the body, soul, and spirit to the world. This happens between ages 9 and 10. At this time children again have a remarkable experience completely unconsciously. However, this unconscious experience is present within them in all kinds of perceptions, feelings, will impulses, and thoughts with perhaps no external connection. Namely, children have this experience: Here is an authority figure who opens up the world to me. I look at the cosmos through this person. Is he or she correct? Is this person giving me a true picture of the world? Make no mistake; I am not saying this is a conscious deliberation. It all plays out in an intimate, delicate way in the world of perception.

But at this point in time it is decided whether or not a child can continue with the right feeling of trust in an authority figure, the kind of trust a child must have up to the time of sexual maturity if he or she is to thrive. This accounts for the inner restlessness, the nervousness, of a child. As a teacher, at this time in a child's life, one must find the words that will further anchor this trust because with this anchoring of trust the moral character of a child is also anchored, which for the time being is still completely latent within his or her organization. But a child is able to stabilize and become internally strong. Children take into their physical body that which was previously absorbed in the described way through their own self.

Today's psychology, which on the one hand is only anthropology and on the other hand abstract psychology, does not take the most important facts into consideration. One can say, up to the time of the change of teeth, all organic formations and functions come from the nerve-sense system. Between the change of teeth and sexual maturity, a child will either become strong and robust or weak and sick through that which takes place in the rhythmic system, in breathing and blood circulation. Between ages 9 and 10 is the point in life when that which previously lodged in the breathing and was still anchored in a human being's upper regions essentially goes over into the blood circulation where inner-organically that brilliant orientation between one and four, between approximately 18 breaths per minute and 72 pulse beats, is implemented. This ratio between breathing and blood circulation establishes itself at this point in time. But this is only the physical expression of deep soul processes. Anchoring of trust between children and teachers must fall into these deep processes of the soul, for thus the stabilization of the inner being also occurs.

This is what one must describe as a particular detail if one wishes to speak about moral education and the relationship of education to the concept of morality. At this time in a child's life, one has knowledge of one of the things through which one is in a position to influence the whole of a person's earthly life either in a positive way as a blessing or in a negative way as a hindrance.

By way of comparison, I would again like to mention how that which one brings to children during this life phase has a continual effect for all of their later life. Perhaps you have already observed there are people who have a remarkable effect on their surroundings when they are elderly. It may be a known fact that such people exist. They really do not need to talk much in the company of others; they just need to be there. Their way of being has an effect of blessing on their surroundings. They bring calm and harmony. What emanates from people at such an age is a gracious blessing. If one has the patience and energy to look from where this gift of blessing comes in later life, one would conclude that someone possesses this gift as a development of a seed placed earlier, and that this seed consisted of the fact that this person, with the deepest respect, looked up to an authority figure in the right way.

Or, I might also say, the person's moral judgment went over into the area of reverence where it gradually rose to the level of religious feeling. If, as a child, between the time of the change of teeth and sexual maturity, one has learned reverence and learned to rise fully into religious feeling—completely lift moral feeling into the light of religious feeling, bring reverence to expression in true prayer— the result of this childhood prayer when one is aged will be that one has the gift of spreading grace and blessing. Figuratively speaking, it can absolutely be said: "Hands that have learned to pray as a child have the gift of reaching out in blessing in later life." This is expressed symbolically, but it illustrates how seeds planted in childhood have an impact on the whole of later life.

Here is an example of how a person's various life stages are interconnected. We already have an example with respect to morality in that we can say, as I have already expressed: The faculty of thinking develops continuously. But with the change of teeth, the memory takes on a different character. In a manner of speaking, the faculty of speech reverses itself. Between the change of teeth and sexual maturity, a child gains a completely different relationship to languages. One can meet this relationship to languages in the right way through a sensible approach to grammar and speech logic. One can do anything as long as, in the first few years of childhood, one does not unreasonably lift up the unconscious aspect of languages into a child's consciousness but rather in a way that takes the child into account.

How is it in respect to the third relationship with which a child comes into balance with the world through the use of his or her entire musculoskeletal system? For most people, the musculo-skeletal system is generally interpreted only in an external, mechanical way. For example, most people do not understand that our whole spatial visualization and mathematical images of the projection of our movements into the limbs, the possibilities of movement, are contained in the intellect. Through the intellect the head experiences that which we, in our humanness, experience as movement. Within the movement mechanism lives something that is deeply a part of the human soul. There is a deep soul element connected with external, material forces. And that which a human being accomplishes in early childhood by going from moving on all fours to standing upright by positioning the spine vertically in relation to Earth's surface—by rising up out of an animal-like posture—this act of raising oneself up is the physical manifestation of a person's moral structure, of his or her moral will forces.

### GA 305, August 16, 1922, Page 21

In this introductory talk today I will point out only this one thing: There is a critical moment for every child during the primary school years, roughly between ages 9 and 11, a moment which must not be overlooked by teachers. At this time between ages 9 and 11 a question arises before the soul of all children (if they are normally developed): "How can I find my way into the world?" One may not assume that the question is put forth just as I have now stated it. It arises within undefined feelings; within feelings of dissatisfaction. The question appears in such a way that a child feels a greater need of dependence upon an adult. Perhaps the question will even appear in the form of a strong infatuation for an adult. But we must understand how to observe correctly what is happening within a child at this critical moment. A child may suddenly feel lonely and isolated and seek a connection. Up to this time he or she has accepted authority as a matter of course. Now, a child begins to ask: What is it with this authority? An enormous amount for the whole of a person's later life depends upon whether or not teachers find the right words at this moment.

Between the years of early childhood, when a child can actually suffer from overstimulation of the nerve-sense system, and the years of adolescence after puberty, are the school years from the change of teeth to sexual maturity. In the middle of all this, as I have described to you, exists the pictorial life of soul. On the exterior is the rhythmic system with respiration and blood circulation working into each other. How respiration and blood circulation internally harmonize, how a child breathes at school and how breathing gradually conforms to blood circulation—all this usually happens between ages 9 and 10. Initially, up to age 9, respiration is predominant. Then, through an inner struggle in the organism, a kind of harmony is produced between pulse and respiration when the blood circulation becomes predominant. This is present in the physical body on the one side and in the mental soul on the other side.

All the child's forces that were gone through during the change of teeth strive toward an inner, plastic, vivid, graphic quality. We can be supportive of this pictorial quality if we convey everything to children using visual imagery. Between ages 9 and 10, something remarkable happens. At this time, much more than before, children want to be "seized" by music and "grabbed" by rhythm. If we observe children and how they receive the musical element up to this point in time, we must recognize how a true inner understanding of the musical element begins to occur between ages 9 and 10. Before that time we observe in children how the musical element really lives plastically and naturally becomes a part of the inner plasticity of the physical body, and also how the musical element extraordinarily easily goes into something dance-like, goes over into movement.

The transition will be very clearly recognizable. Naturally these things are not so strictly delineated. Those who can see and understand will still cultivate the musical element in children before age 9, but in the correct way, tending more toward the aspect that I have just characterized. Otherwise, between ages 9 and 10, children would get a shock if the musical element suddenly approached and internally grabbed hold of them since they are absolutely not accustomed to being so strongly internally influenced in this way.

## GA 306, April 18, 1923, Page 88

One must bring this to children with a certain amount of finesse and practice, artful educational practice, so that they are not conventionally drilled to repeat the letters of the alphabet, but rather experience the alphabet letters coming into being, what lies in their formative forces, what they really have there. Upon this it depends. And then we will see that it is plenty good enough if, in this way, we can bring children to the point of being able to read by shortly after age 9. As a matter of fact, it does not hurt anything if they cannot read earlier. One can say children have learned to read in a natural way if it happens a few months past age 9 and has been taught in the way I have just described. With individual children it can be somewhat earlier or later.

That is to say, a minor phase of life begins for children at this time. The major epochs have been mentioned many times: from birth up to the change of teeth, from the change of teeth up to sexual maturity, and into the 20s. However, today one absolutely may not speak of further development into the 20s! It is true, is it not, that today it is not acceptable to say to a person: "You still go through a phase of development up to a specific stage of maturity after age 21." That offends a person of today. He is not developing, he is writing feature articles. Today, one must be a little cautious when speaking of the later years. However, as teachers and educators, it is important to understand about the major developmental epochs as well as the minor phases that occur within them. There is a shorter phase between ages 9 and 10, situated closer to age 9, when children come more and more to differentiating from their environment. This is the first time they are really aware of being "I." Therefore, before this time, that which one brings to children through education must be brought in such a way that they grow together with their surroundings as much as possible. Until this age children cannot at all differentiate, as "I," from their surroundings.

**Page 90f.**

Definitions are, of course, very useful, but also almost always very one-sided. However, the main thing is that one finds one's way straight into life. I must always repeat this. The important thing is that, above all, one realizes that up until after age 9 a child really does not distinguish his or her own self from the environment. So, one actually cannot say that if a child hits a table, he or she imagines it to be a living thing. That would never occur to a child. The hitting comes from out of the child's inner being. Animism, or the ensouling of inorganic objects, has already slipped into our cultural history, but it does not really exist. One is completely amazed at what fantasies academics often have when they believe, for example, that human beings enliven objects.

Whole mythologies are thus explained. When people declare things like this, it is as if they had never become acquainted with a primitive person. For instance, a farmer, if he is also still primitive, would never have the idea to ensoul or enliven natural phenomena. It has to do with the fact that children do not possess the concept of "ensouling" or "enlivening" objects. As a child lives, so lives everything, but there is no conscious dreaming oneself into objects. Therefore, you must not point out any differences when you are describing the surroundings: You must let the plants live. You must let everything live because a child does not yet differentiate his or her "I" from the environment.

For this reason, during these childhood years until after age 9, you also cannot yet approach children, for example, with anything containing an intellectualized description. In full freshness and vigor you must transform everything into images, pictures. When the picture stops and the description begins, one accomplishes absolutely nothing at ages 8 or 9. Only later is this possible. And then, again, it has to do with one finding one's way correctly into these specific phases of life. Only for pictorial representations does a child have any understanding at all up to age 9. The other is more than a child is capable of comprehending, just as the eye cannot perceive sound.

However, between ages 9 and 10 you can begin to, let us say, describe plants. You can begin there with primitive descriptions of plants because children are gradually learning to differentiate from the environment. However, you cannot yet describe anything in the mineral kingdom because their ability to differentiate is not yet so strong that they are able to grasp the great difference between that which is experienced internally and the mineral element. At first, children have only the ability to understand the difference between their own self and a plant. Then you can gradually transition into animal descriptions.

## Page 92

You should not directly approach children with that which comes out of today's botany and bring that into the classroom. One should describe the plants and earth from real life, just as one would describe the hair that grows out of a person's head. Actually, you should not describe the plants at all without also talking about the sunshine, climate, and Earth configuration in a way suited to children's understanding.

## Page 93f.

With botany during the childhood years, we must approach it from the standpoint of the whole Earth, viewing plants as "hair" that grows upon the Earth.

Regarding animals—yes, children gain absolutely no relationship to the animal kingdom if you develop the idea of coexistence, side by side but separate from human beings. In this regard you can expect little more from children since the study of animals begins at around ages 10 or 11. Teaching children about animals in such a way that they appear side by side, coexisting in a parallel configuration is certainly very good from a scientific standpoint, but from the standpoint of reality, it is not a good idea. That is to say, in reality, the whole animal kingdom is like an unfurled, spread-out human being.

Look at a lion, for instance. A lion is the one-sidedly developed chest organization of the human being. Look at an elephant. Its whole organization is formed upon the lengthening of the upper lip. Look at a giraffe. Its whole organization is formed upon the lengthening of the neck. If you comprehend every animal in this way—that any human organ system is one-sidedly developed in an animal—and then survey all the animals down to the insects—and this can be taken even further down to the geologic animals (*Terebratula*, essentially, are not geologic animals)—you will come to the point where you say the whole animal kingdom is a fan-shaped, unfolded human being and the human being, in his or her physical organization, is the whole animal kingdom folded together. Thus, with the right distance from the human being, and, on the other hand, also with the right connection to the human being, you bring to the children that which the animal kingdom is in reality.

Of course, I am saying in a few words something that is quite abstract. You must translate it into something alive and vivid so you can present every animal species as a one-sided development of a human organ system. If you can muster the necessary energy to present this to children in this lively way, you will see how quickly they grasp the idea. That is what you want to happen. Plants are tied to the Earth as if they are the Earth's "hair." Animals are associated with the human being insofar as you look at them as if the human being were one-sidedly developed; as if someone were suddenly all arms, or legs, nose, upper lip, etc., and then these aspects gained form. That is how one arrives at the form of an animal, of the whole animal kingdom. In this way one succeeds in creating lessons so they are related to that which lives in children.

**GA 306, April 19, 1923, Page 95ff.**

Above all, what must be considered in educational practice during a child's seventh year is that one is able to correctly orient oneself to, and within, the feeling life of a child. It is really a question of creating the right imagery and pictorial concepts which can lead children through the delicate transitions that exist during this period of life.

When one receives children into school, there is something that continues to function in accordance with the earlier physical-religious disposition, as I have called it. It is a longing to sense and perceive everything that is happening in the surroundings. This perception, which goes over into imitation, then unites itself with attentive listening to how the teacher, with his or her natural, self-evident authority, is affecting a child. During this time in childhood it absolutely must be that "true" is not that which has been investigated for truth, but rather that which a natural-authority figure has said is true. Likewise, something must be untrue for the same reason—a natural-authority figure finds it to be untrue. It is the same with "beautiful" and "ugly" and "good" and "bad." One can arrive at an independent and free judgment or opinion about right and wrong, good and bad, beautiful and ugly in later life only if, at this age, one has been able, with deep reverence, to look up to an authority figure in regard to these things.

Naturally, this may not be a forced, commanded authority. It may not be an externally established authority. At least, if, for external social reasons, the authority is ordered and externally established, the children may not be made aware of that. Through children's sense of their own feelings and perceptions they must get an impression from a teacher that prompts them to look up to that person as the appropriate authority. One must preserve and sustain everything in this tender authoritative relationship, especially between the ages of 7 and 9; that is, from the beginning of primary school up to age 9. One must sustain it over a long period of time, but it modifies itself between ages 9 and 10.

Something else comes together with a child's natural, matter-of-course, settling into this authoritative relationship. In the first seven-year epoch up to the change of teeth, children are sense-beings. In a certain way they are totally a sense-organ. But, a sense-organ by which, with every move, the will takes effect. It may seem strange to you that I say children are a sense organ in which the will works. But it only seems strange to you because today's psychology, and what it has produced in the way of popular thinking and notions, is something completely inadequate. Today, one does not normally think about the will when one thinks about eyes, for instance. However, regarding eyes, it is a fact that the will-aspect brings about the inner picture and not something else. In every sense organ the will-aspect creates an inner image. A sense organ which is passive has initially simply the task of revealing itself or people in the outside world. But within every sense organ, inner activity takes place which is of a will-nature. Children's will-aspect works intensively throughout their physical body up until the change of teeth, although it still remains available. Namely, between entry into primary school and approximately age 9, the will-aspect at first can only tolerate being introduced to all things about nature and human beings if one does it in a very human-oriented, pictorial way.

For example, we work in such a way that we actually do not bring an aesthetic, but rather, an artistic element right into the first lessons. We let the children busy themselves with color. From the very beginning we just let them handle color, even if it is sometimes quite inconvenient in the classroom. We let the children busy themselves with color because by doing so they follow their own forces of imagery in putting the colors down side by side. They have the gratification of putting color next to color, nothing significant, but rather instinctive-meaningful, putting color next to color. They even develop a wonderfully instinctive way of putting the colors next to each other. One can already see how this putting together of color can be directed into drawing and how it can lead into writing.

During these years children remain completely without understanding of the fact that one wishes to explain something to them. A child has no understanding of this. If one wishes to explain something, it will dull children. That does not work at all. However, it goes wonderfully well if everything that one wishes to bring to them is told as a narrative rather than as explanation. When a teacher paints with words and ideas, brings rhythm into teaching, has music not only in music class but as an ever present musical and rhythmic element presiding over, children have a very fine understanding of this. But if one describes things to children concerning aspects of human will and feeling, they will resist that. That is to say, between entry into primary school and age 9, children will bristle at any attempt to describe and explain about human beings. Children would tremendously resist that; they could hardly stand it. Handling everything in a way that is oriented toward human beings, even down to the inorganic creatures of nature, is something a child's inner being actually demands at this time.

Children's horror, as one could call it, of descriptions of human beings remains up to around age 12. We can very well implement that which I talked about yesterday between ages 9 and 12. As I explained yesterday, we can present the plant kingdom to children as hair that grows on the Earth, but we must remain consistent with the metaphoric characteristics. We also can bring the animal kingdom closer to children by regarding every animal as a single part of the human being that has one-sidedly developed. But we may certainly not transition into anything like a description of human beings at this time. It would even be very good to tell children we are talking about elements of the human being and that these elements are developed one-sidedly and belong to this or that kind of animal. But the aggregation, the coming together of all these elements in the human being, is not yet understood by children. Around age 12 children begin to have a longing to bring together the whole animal kingdom relative to human beings. One can then begin to study this in those classes when children are between ages 11 and 12.

Herein lies an apparent contradiction, but life is full of contradictions. The seeming contradiction is that one should first describe the whole animal kingdom as an unfolded human being. However, it is still correct to do it this way before one depicts human beings as occupying a place in the compendium. In a certain way children must first get a feeling for everything to do with human characteristics inhabiting the whole Earth as one-sidedly developed living creatures and that the world of animals, in singular examples, are one-sidedly developed aspects of a whole human being. Then children must experience the great moment when one summarizes how all that is unfolded and spread out in the animal world is concentrated in the human being. This is what your teaching is all about, that one allows children to really experience decisive moments in life. That is to say, one lets this be infused in their soul: The essence and the combined summation of the whole animal world is, on a higher level, the human being as a physical being.

At this age it does not matter if one teaches this or that knowledge from grade level to grade level. What matters is that one lets children really experience decisive moments in life, lets them climb over certain childhood "mountains of human existence," if I may express it that way. This has an effect on the whole of later life. In our times, because of the way things have developed scientifically, there is very little talent for looking so intimately at a human life and a human being.

**Page 109ff.**

In a manner of speaking, a child travels with his or her soul the whole way from the inside to the outside. Until around age 12 children really cannot absorb it if one describes human beings to them. Around age 12 they begin to process conceptual descriptions of human beings and look at themselves in the mirror of the world. At this time children are able to abide their own self when one explains about what human beings are. There is a complete turnabout in human nature from the change of teeth to puberty.

Within this time period there is a very important life transition. For most children it occurs between ages 9 and 10, depending on the individual. With some children it happens after age 10. For all children something happens whereby they stand instinctively and unconsciously before one of life's mysteries. This turnaround from the inside to the outside and awareness that one is an "I" and that the world is outside—which was all interwoven before—is something children do not consciously experience. But what they experience is inner doubt and disquiet; those things make an appearance. In the physical body this is expressed in such a way that during this moment in life, breathing actually aligns precisely with blood circulation for the first time. It balances itself out and human beings produce the appropriate ratio between pulse and breathing. This is the physical correlation for something that is soul/spiritual. At this moment in life children especially need us as teachers and educators. There is an appeal to teachers at this time which does not come in the form of a question but rather as a kind of behavior.

Children now want to present us with the great questions of life and we must acquire the educational finesse to be able to weigh these things correctly in each individual case. What are these life questions? Up to this point the taken-for-granted relationship of authority between teacher and child has developed in such a way that a teacher is actually the child's world. For children, the stars move because they know the teacher knows the stars move. Everything is good and bad, pretty and ugly, true and false because the teacher thinks so. Everything that comes from the world, in a certain sense, must go through the teacher; that is the only healthy state of things. Between ages 9 and 10, sometimes a little later, a question arises before a child's soul, not in defined terms and concepts, but in feelings and perceptions: From where does my teacher get all of this? If I may offer this image: Teachers suddenly start to become transparent. One wants to see the world that is standing behind a teacher and lives behind him or her. Teachers must withstand this. In the face of what a child brings to them at this time, they must maintain in this child the belief that they are really correctly joined with the world and carry truth, beauty, and goodness inside them. I would say that the unconscious nature of a child tests a teacher in a completely awful way. Children test teachers to see if they really carry the world inside them and if they were worthy to be the representative for the whole cosmos.

On the other hand, children are unable to verbalize this because causality makes no sense to them. If one were to, in any form, even only hint at showing this theoretically through reasons, causes, or something similar, the unconscious nature of the children would perceive it as weakness in a teacher and not strength, only as weakness. Everything which one must first prove already lives only faintly in the soul. That which lives strongly in the soul, one must not first prove. This also applies to cultural development.

I will not make a determination now as to content, but I would like to introduce you to the dynamics of the matter: Up to a certain point in time in the Middle Ages, people knew what *The Last Supper* represented. At that time one was not yet touched by the necessity of proof. Suddenly people began to sense the necessity of proof relative to *The Last Supper*. For those who saw through the matter, this was only proof that the people no longer understood anything about *The Last Supper*. One does not need evidence that someone is a thief if one has seen that person stealing something. If one has seen him, one simply refers to him as a thief. Evidence is always related to that which one does not know, but never to that which one truly knows through the events of life itself. That is why it is ludicrous when people try to find a connection between formal logic and reality. It is like searching for a connection between the path that leads to a mountain and the mountain itself. That is to say, the path is there so that I get to the mountain, then the mountain begins. Logic is there only so that one comes to reality. Reality begins where logic ends.

Yes, that one understands these things oneself is of completely fundamental importance. One may not fall into the error of wanting to prove to a child during this important time in life that one is the right representative of the world. Rather, one must now, through a new demeanor and different behavior, instill in a child the direct sensation of belief: Yes, the teacher knows a lot more than I thought! Then children realize teachers can grow, they have not yet shown all their sides, and they are not yet spent. Perhaps a teacher will say something one on one that surprises a child so they again unconsciously sense and listen to this new aspect of what has been heard for the first time from the teacher. This is when the right relationship has been established. One must preserve something within oneself and, above all, for this point in time one must be able to preserve something within oneself whereby, as a teacher, one can rise in a child's estimation.

This is the solution to an important riddle of life at this moment: that, for a child and his or her perceptual sense, one can increase; one suddenly grows over and above oneself. This is the solace and strength that one must give a child at this moment in life—because he or she has already approached the teacher with this request and already developed the necessary love and favor. Teachers who are unaware of this will have the bitter experience, when a child is between ages 9 and 10, of seeing their authority gradually dissipate until it is no longer there. Then these teachers will try something terrible; they will try, with evidence, to prove everything, and the like.

### GA 307, August 11, 1923, Page 135ff.

The greatest Divine revelation is a developing human being. If one learns to know about growing human beings, not merely the anatomical-physiological aspects, one learns how soul and spirit flow down into the physical body. Then any knowledge of human beings transforms itself into religiosity, into devotional, awed reverence before that which streams into the temporal surface from Divine depths. This is how we receive that which supports and sustains us as teachers, and what children already sense, that which becomes dedication and natural authority.

As teachers, instead of taking a paddle in hand—or an inner paddle which creates inner hurt, as I explained yesterday—instead of arming ourselves with a paddle, so to speak, we should much more arm ourselves with true knowledge of human beings, true observation of human beings, which transitions into moral-religious inner experience and moral-religious reverence before God's creation. Then we have our proper position within the school and also realize something that is absolutely necessary for all education: There are certain moments to be observed in a human life when a person stands at a turning point, a metamorphosis of life. Such a metamorphosis occurs between ages 9 and 10. With one child it may be earlier and with another a little later, but as a rule it occurs between ages 9 and 10.

Materialists and rationalists lightly pass over things such as this. But if one has a sense for true observation of human beings, one sees how, at this age between 9 and 10, something remarkable happens with every child. Children become outwardly a little restless; they cannot come to terms with the outside world. They feel something which prompts them to become timid and reserved, causing them to withdraw slightly from the outside world. This happens in an intimate, subtle way with almost every child. If it does not occur, the child is abnormal. We must observe that between ages 9 and 10 an extraordinarily important question arises as a feeling in a child. The child cannot translate this question into a concept or notion nor express it in words. Everything is a feeling but, even so, the feeling is all the stronger and it wants to be considered all the more intensely. What do children want at this age?

Until now, from out of a natural impulse, children have revered teachers. But children become uncertain. Now they feel teachers must, in some special way, show they are worthy of that reverence. As teachers it is essential when we notice this happening with a child that we respond through our attitude and behavior, but it does not have to be anything contrived. For instance, we may be especially kind and attentive in our dealings with a child, make a special point of speaking to an individual child, so he or she realizes our affection and sympathy. If we watch for this moment between ages 9 and 10 and act accordingly, a child is saved from a precipice, so to speak. The fact that we help a child through this period is of enormous importance for the whole of his or her later life because whatever remains in the form of insecurity will reappear as insecurity for the rest of someone's life, albeit in such a way that it is not noticeable. It reappears and expresses itself in a person's character, temperament, and physical health.

Above all, we must understand how spirit works in the physical body and how it must be nurtured so it can beneficially influence physical health. The art of education shows just how much we must penetrate and understand the cooperation between spirit and physical matter as harmonious and never as in opposition to each other. We must recognize how much we owe to this art of education which is in direct contradiction to our modern civilization which has separated everything.

## GA 310, July 20, 1924, Page 72f.

We cannot introduce children too soon to the artistic element; all of our teaching must be permeated with it. We must keep in mind that, just as the etheric body is accounted as containing the pictorial, formative forces, so the astral body, which underlies the life of feeling and perception, is organized around a human being's musical nature. What must we look for when we observe children? Deep inside, a mentally healthy child is musical because between the change of teeth and puberty the astral body is still embedded in the physical and etheric bodies. Every healthy child is musical deep inside. We must only call forth this musical aspect from out of a child's own movements and activities. For this reason teaching that makes use of the arts, both the visual arts and musical arts, should be cultivated from the beginning of school life. The abstract may not dominate here; rather, the artistic element must prevail. Children must be led into understanding the world from out of the artistic element.

We must proceed in such a way that children gradually learn to find their place in the world. As I have said before, it is an abhorrent sight to see someone carry today's scholarly textbooks into the classroom and then prepare the lessons according to those books. Today, in our academic pursuits, which I fully acknowledge, we have deviated in many respects from a natural view of the world.

We will now ask ourselves this question: At approximately what age can one begin to teach children about the world of plants? This must be done neither too late nor too early. One must understand clearly that between ages 9 and 10 is a very important period in a child's development. Those who see with a pedagogical eye observe this in every child. There comes a time when a child, not through speaking, but rather through his or her whole demeanor, indicates that there is a question or a number of questions which betray an inner crisis. This is an extraordinarily subtle experience for a child, and to pick up on it requires an extraordinarily subtle sense of perception. But it is there and it must be observed. At this age a child learns quite instinctively to differentiate from the outside world. Before this time, the "I" and the outside world flow into each other and one can tell stories about animals and plants and rocks as if they behaved like people. It is best to appeal to children's pictorial understanding and talk about the whole of the natural world in this way. Between ages 9 and 10 children learn to fully consciously say "I" when referring to their own self. They learned to say this earlier, of course, but now it is with full consciousness. In these years when a child, with his or her consciousness, no longer flows into the outside world but rather learns to differentiate from it, this is the point in time when we also can begin to teach understanding of the plant world without immediately abandoning the pictorial approach, understanding permeated with feeling.

**GA 310, July 24, 1924, Page 150f.**

Take, for example, the method of teaching history. To teach history to children before they are age 9 or 10 is a completely absurd proposition, for they have absolutely no ability to become "historical" in their outlook. Beginning at age 9 or 10—just observe this for yourself —children start to become interested in individual people. If you place historical figures like Caesar, or Achilles, Hector, Agamemnon, or Alcibiades in the foreground as self-contained personalities, allowing the rest of the history surrounding these individuals to appear only in the background, and you paint the whole thing in this way, children will have the greatest interest in it. They get the urge to delve into biographies of historical figures if you depict them in this way. Self-contained portraits of historical figures—pictures of how a meal looked in a certain century and how it looked in another century, how people ate before there were forks, how a person ate in Ancient Rome; how people in Ancient Greece walked, how with every step they were conscious of what the leg was as a form, how they felt the form; and in contrast how the people of the Old Testament, the Hebrews, walked, they who had absolutely no feeling for the form, but let their arms and legs dangle, as it were—all this elicits a sense for these details that can be brought into the picture. This is what the teaching of history should entail between ages 10 and 12.

### GA 313, April 14, 1921, Page 69ff.

In some of the general lectures, when I spoke about linguistics (I could not accommodate the topic in the natural sciences section, but it would have been just as well-suited there), I said that the specific, particular processes from out of the organism that express themselves more outwardly during puberty and are discharged more inwardly from birth to the change of teeth (during which time a human being acquires speech), the processes that take place between the astral body and the etheric body, and also the physical body, underlie the acquisition of speech and all the changes in the human organism that are associated with learning to speak. These are the processes that should be carefully observed in children. Changes in the rest of the physical organism always run parallel with a child's learning to speak.

As I have said before, one should not only observe the changes going forward, after birth, but also one should look backward from the radical transformation at the time of the change of teeth to the child's learning speech. But now there is an equally significant transformation that lies ahead which is henceforward turned inward and does not announce itself quite so externally as the change of teeth or the acquisition of speech, for instance, which transformations anyone can observe because they are expressed outwardly. In any event, a change lies ahead, one that is almost more important relative to human health and illness than the others.

I would say that in child-rearing, instinctively, much more is made of the earlier changes because things develop out in the open. Actually, something of much greater significance underlies this other process that plays out in the time between the change of teeth and puberty. It is the process that lies directly midway between those two events, and it has to do with the true "I," that, as I have already explained, is in that sense first born exoterically—completely exoterically, I would say— around age 20. The "I" is now also born inwardly, just as the astral body is with the acquisition of speech. The process reaches its culmination between ages 9 and 10.

At this time you must consider the following: That which is intrinsically characteristic to human beings with respect to the ego, or "I," is almost never taken into consideration. The "I," as something that lives within a human organism, does something very special. Everything else in a human being—the physical (to an even greater extent, but I will come back to that), the etheric, and also the astral (which only through oxygen is connected outwardly to that which is immediately outside of a human being)—all are part of the human essence; they are actually quite strongly linked to inner aspects of the human being.

During sleep the astral body is almost the only thing from a human organism that the "I" takes with it. The astral body has a very strong affinity with the physical, and, specifically, with the etheric body. That is not the case with the "I." Relative to the "I," namely, its relationship to the outside world, the deep difference between human beings and animals is so clearly indicated. By taking in nourishment we are feeding ourselves substances that are also substances in the outside world. These substances must be transformed within human beings. Who brings about this thorough transformation of outer substances within human beings? Who does this? In truth, it is the "I," the ego. The ego alone is powerful enough, in a manner of speaking, to stretch its feelers all the way down into the forces of outer substances.

Schematically speaking, let me say, an outer substance has certain forces that must be de-combined, or de-constructed, if they are to be changed and recombined within a human organism. The etheric and astral bodies only skirt around the substances, so to speak. They have no power to penetrate to the inner aspect of substances but simply skirt around them. It is the "I" alone that really has anything to do with penetrating down and going into the substances themselves. When you deliver a food substance to a human organism, at first, it is inside the person. However, the "I" overrides the whole human organism and goes directly into the food substance. An interaction occurs between a person's ego and the inner forces of food substance. Here, two things overlap one another: the outer world as it relates to chemistry and physics and the inner world of human beings with its preference for what is anti-chemistry and physics. That is the essence of the matter.

It is a fact that with a child, actually up to the time of the beginning of the change of teeth, this penetration into the substance of matter is regulated by the head. Children are born in such a way that, by an indirect route through the head during embryonic development, forces are given that are active in human beings for the purpose of processing matter from the inside out. But in the period of time after the change of teeth up to puberty, with the culmination being between ages 9 and 10, the part of the ego that works from out of the lower being, the lower "I," must now meet up with the higher "I." With a child it is always the "I" that works out of the higher being that still processes the substances of matter up to this time period that I have characterized. Naturally, I mean the "tools" of the ego. The "I" is, of course, an integrated whole. But the tools of the "I," the polarity of the "I," that is, the lower "I" that meets up with the upper "I," begins to come into proper relationship during the time I have indicated. That is to say, at this time, the "I" must enter into the human organization, just as the astral body must join itself with the human organization when a child learns to speak.

With these presuppositions in mind, observe all the occurrences that happen in children from 8 or 9 years old up to around 12 or 13 years old, just those occurrences that are so important to observe in the primary school years. Take a look at these occurrences from this viewpoint: They find their outer expression in a searching of the human organism. This searching consists of looking for harmony between the material substances that are ingested and the inner human organization that can be first established only during physical life. Carefully observe if, during this time, the head will not correctly take in the inner forces of material substance. If the head refuses, observe how this expresses itself as a headache in children around ages 9, 10, and 11. Then observe how the accompanying symptoms appear in the form of problems with metabolism, secretion of gastric acid, and so on. Observe all of this and you will see how some children are, in a manner of speaking, continually ill because of insufficient attunement of the lower and upper "I."

If one keeps a careful eye on such things, one gets through them and they usually disappear. They fade away after puberty, at which time the astral body is in attendance and harmonizes whatever the "I" is unable to bring into alignment. Between ages 14 to 15 and 20 to 21, this slowly abates. Children who are susceptible to illness between the change of teeth and puberty can later become extraordinarily healthy. There is something very informative about this. You may have already found that sickly children, namely those whose illness is outwardly manifested in the form of problems with irregular digestion, with careful treatment, later become very healthy individuals.

It is especially important that great care is exercised in prescribing a diet. Amazing progress can be made in this direction if parents and teachers of children with this kind of ailment do not continually serve them all kinds of rich food and constantly try to coax them with it. That only makes things worse. Try to fathom what the child can digest well and give those foods to the child in small portions. Divide the daily food intake into many smaller meals. One will then see what a great service can be done for such children in this way. To believe that something can be accomplished by overfeeding and the like is a completely false assumption.

If one also sees to it that such children are not overloaded with homework, thereby worsening the condition, and also that they get the proper amount of rest, one has, additionally, assisted to meet the demands of the necessary digestive activity required in response to smaller portions of food. There is hardly any other area in which more transgressions are made, in relation to which the above suggestions are made. One can say with certainty that if one does not make sure of healthy human development in this regard, something from the tendencies to illness at this age will remain and cause all sorts of dispositions to illness for the rest of a person's life.

People very easily complain that in the Waldorf school we are extraordinarily sparing when it comes to assigning homework. We have good reason for this. An educational system in accordance with reality does not only look to abstract objectives or abstractions in general, which prevail in many areas of life today. A reality-based educational system takes everything into consideration that should be considered in genuine human development. Above all, what belongs in those considerations is that one does not torment children with homework because essentially, homework is sometimes the hidden cause of a bad digestion at a later life stage. These things may first manifest themselves later, but they are still thoroughly effective. Typically, a supersensible study of human development indicates that what is prepared in an earlier life stage foretells occurrence in later life stages.

The danger of the linkage, if I may put it that way, of the "I" into a human organism exists from below. This danger is actually extraordinarily great for almost all people in our society when they are children and, for this reason, one should take these things into consideration with everyone unless they happen to be extremely well-grounded. Most people today are very highly susceptible to the dangers that come from the "I" being poorly joined with the organism, which is basically ruined before this joining can take place. They are susceptible to the dangers that occur precisely with this linking of the "I" with the organism.

From out of the respiratory system, and also the head system, females are more sensitive to the typically unstable equilibrium that is present. Relative to the chest organization, males are not more stable, but more robust or less sensitive, one could say. Actually, the same damages can occur, but they are less manifest in males than in females. Females are more sensitive to everything that occurs in this regard, and that which I have described, the searching for the correct linking with the "I," is resolved in either a healthy human being or in one with anemia. Anemia is the direct continuation of everything of this kind that has occurred in an abnormal way from age 7 onward. Anemia does not assert itself until later but it is actually just the intensification of everything that took place in this direction at an earlier age but was still imperceptible.

I must point out something that it is extraordinarily important to differentiate. If you look at the circulatory system, there must be a distinction made between the actual circulation, which is a sum of movements, and that which puts itself intimately together with it, that which, in a certain way, inserts itself into blood circulation. It is metabolism. The balance between metabolism and the rhythmic system is definitely achieved by the circulatory system, while the balance between the rhythmic organism and the nerve-sense organism is achieved by the respiratory organism. If you contemplate this middle aspect of the human being, the "chest-being," you certainly will notice that it is organized into two aspects as a polarity. Through breathing it is oriented toward the head, and through blood circulation is it oriented toward the metabolic-limb system.

## Page 77

If you proceed correctly from the viewpoint of the entry of the "I" into outer substances, you will be able to, I would say, penetrate and see through that which you are confronted with in the form of symptoms. You see, if you look back on what I have said over the past few days and what I have emphasized at other times as well, the human organism is not simply something that can be drawn with lines; that is only the fixed aspect. Essentially, the human organism is also organized liquid, organized air, and organized warmth. The "I" must now also join with the various elements of this organization. The linking of the "I" into the warmth conditions of the physical body is also especially important as well as subtle. The "I" must join into the warmth conditions of the body in the following way:

Initially, when a person is born, we have only a copy, an imprint, of the ego, or the "I." I have said before that the copy of the "I" is present in the head. So, we have the copy of the "I" and this is what is active in childhood. In addition, the "I" must now give, I would say, its "being" from below upward; here it must join in. This is expressed internally in such a way that the copy of the "I" we have in our head permeates the organism with warmth during the childhood years. This has something to do with the human organism being suffused with warmth. But the permeation of warmth follows a descending curve. It is strongest at birth, insofar as the warming process proceeds from out of the head, and then it follows a descending curve. As human beings, what has developed in the warming curve is necessary in later life for us to maintain at its highest point on the curve, from below upward, through the "I" intervening in the warmth conditions. Later, we must counteract the descending curve with one that is ascending, and which, essentially, depends upon the "I" capturing the rising substantive forces gained through nourishment, and crossing over into the circulation, respiration, and finally into the head system.

# Advice for Teachers and Educators for Age 9/10

**GA 77a, July 28, 1921, Page 90f.**

There are things one should teach children simply on the basis of authority. One cannot teach everything on the basis of visual instruction, such as moral concepts, for instance. In that case one can rely on neither visual instruction nor mere dictates and precepts, but only on one's own self-evident authority. One of the most meaningful experiences one can have in later life comes from having accepted something at age 8, 9, or 12 because a highly respected person viewed it as the truth. Such a relationship with a revered person belongs in the category of the imponderables of teaching and education.

Let us say one has become 30 years old and a certain experience brings up this memory out of the depths of consciousness about something that was accepted as truth actually 20 years ago or more. One finally understands something of what was accepted on authority all those years before. This holds tremendous significance for one's life. In fact it shows how something that was accepted on authority years earlier grows into one's later life in a living way. For this reason all the discussion about whether to have more or less of a visual element is not so important. Things must simply unfold out of themselves. The discussion about whether to have more or less of an intellectual, thinking element, and so on, is even less important. The important thing is that teachers occupy their rightful place in the school and the human aspect is correctly merged with administrative aspects of the school organization. This is where you should mainly focus for your aim and purpose.

**Page 98**

One can lead children into a feeling for Christian sensibilities only beginning at age 8, or even more toward age 9. At this time they begin to understand what is behind the figure of Jesus Christ, for example. Children are just now beginning to grow into understanding the ideas you must teach for a correct understanding of the Gospels. It is good if a foundation is already present and they are appropriately introduced to the Gospels at around age 9, gradually continuing into the deeper mysteries of Christianity. It must be emphasized that the non-church-affiliated religion classes are, in the highest sense, Christian through and through and that those of various denominations taking part in these classes are introduced to true Christianity. It is really true that one comes to be convinced of Christianity if one is a Waldorf teacher, albeit from an anthroposophical viewpoint. One comes into Christianity through the perspective of anthroposophy. Perhaps one will use different words, but the children are introduced to true Christianity. Just as we leave the Protestant and Catholic religious instruction completely free in their approach, so also is the non-church-affiliated religious instruction based on anthroposophy completely free.

**GA 218, November 19, 1922, Page 234**

Between the ages of 9 and 10 something extraordinarily important begins to stir in children. Teachers who are true observers of human beings know that sometime between ages 9 and 10 children have a strong need for something. They do not have intellectualized doubt, but experience inner restlessness. There is something of an inner question present that children cannot verbalize, nor do they need to verbalize it. They feel something dream-like, half unconscious. However, they know exactly that they want something very special from a teacher whom they look up to with love. Normally, one also cannot answer in the same way as one would an intellectualized question. It has much more to do with building up an especially intense and personal relationship of trust so that one calls forth the notion in a child that at this time one speaks a lot more to him or her in an especially loving way.

Within this perception of love and trust in a teacher lies the answer to one of childhood's questions about life of the greatest significance. Of what does this great question consist? As I said, a child does not ask the question with his or her conscious mind, but with the feeling-nature and with the whole subconscious being. We must recognize that up to this age children naïvely and readily accept the authority of a beloved teacher. Now the need arises to perceive "good" and "bad" in a new way, as if they were present in the world as forces. Before, children looked up to a teacher, but now, in a manner of speaking, they want to look through a teacher and be able to think: This teacher is not only the person who says something is good or bad, but it is said because he or she is a messenger of the Spirit, a messenger of God; the teacher's knowledge comes from higher worlds.

As I said, children do not say this with the conscious mind, but they feel it. And a child's specific question, which also arises through feelings, tells a teacher: Such and such is appropriate for this child. This approach will cause that of which one says it is "good" or "bad" or "true" or "false" to take deep root in the child so that he or she gains new trust.

This is also the period of time when one can transition into something other than mere imitation or saying something is good or bad when it comes to teaching moral concepts. At this time one can begin to introduce moral concepts to children in a pictorial way, without engaging the intellect, because that is the approach most suited to children of this age. During primary school, from the change of teeth to puberty, one must absolutely teach children through the use of imagery, through pictures for all the senses. Even though a child is no longer completely a sense-organ, so to speak, he or she still lives in the senses, which now reveal themselves in the visible, physical body.

**Page 235ff.**

When children have reached the point in time between ages 9 and 10, we may begin to introduce pictures that, above all, inspire the imagination—pictures of good people that will elicit feelings of sympathy for what they do. Please notice I did not say one should lecture children about moral precepts. I do not say that one should approach the intellect with moral convictions. One should approach the imagination, the aesthetic sense. One should awaken a feeling of favor or disapproval for good and bad, right and wrong, the noble, honest and ethical deeds, and for world-induced, balancing recompense for wrong actions. Before, one had to place oneself in front of the children as a moral compass, but now one must add pictures which affect nothing other than the active imaginative faculty within the sense-nature. At first, up until puberty, children should absorb moral concepts as feelings. They should be firm in their conviction of feeling: This is something for which I have sympathy, the good; this is something for which I have antipathy, the bad. Sympathy and antipathy, judgments of feelings, should be the foundation of moral concepts.

If one sees, as I have presented it, that the human organism is something in which everything is connected and interrelated, one will realize it is a matter of doing the right thing for a child at the right time. You could not let a plant grow in such a way that it would go directly into flowering. First the plant must be established in its roots. The flowering must happen later. If you wanted to turn the root into a flower, that would be nonsense. If you wanted to teach children between the change of teeth and puberty intellectually-formulated moral concepts, it would be as if you wanted to turn the root of a plant into a flower. First, you must care for the seed, that is to say, the root, or moral concepts, in the form of feelings.

If a child has tended the moral concepts within the feeling-nature, he or she will awaken to intelligence, or thinking-nature, after puberty. A child will continue that which appeared as feelings between the change of teeth and puberty through inner development that takes place through to sexual maturity. Then intellectual moral concepts can awaken. This is something that is so important in life that all teaching of moral concepts must be based upon it! Just as you cannot turn a plant's root into a flower, but must wait until the root develops and the plant finally develops into a flower, so you must, in a manner of speaking, tend the moral root in a child's feelings of judgment and feelings of sympathy for what is moral. Then you must let someone carry his or her feelings into the intellect through the human power within his or her own being. The person will have a deep, inner sense of satisfaction when in later life he or she will not merely have memories of what a teacher said, that something was morally right or wrong, but rather the person will live with inner happiness, inner strength that fills his or her entire life of soul because there was an awakening to forming moral judgments and opinions at the right time in complete freedom.

### GA 297, August 31, 1919, Page 48ff.

At age 9 or thereabouts, everything begins to develop that makes children capable of coming out of the human realm a little more and learning about nature, albeit still from a human perspective. Before this time children are not really capable of grasping nature as such. I would say, however, that up to age 9 children are very capable of looking at the world in a moralizing way. Teachers must meet a child's desire for morality without becoming pedantic.

Certainly something of this kind, in this direction, was already present somewhat instinctively. If one goes through the tutorials on educational methods currently available that lean toward all subject matter being oriented toward a human aspect, one could be driven to despair. A certain correct instinct is there, but the instructions given for this age group are almost without exception pervaded by philistinism and banality that is terribly harmful to a becoming human being. That is to say, at this age, one does well to examine animals and plants only in such a way that a certain morality shines through from the observation, such as if one tells fables to children in such a way that they learn about the animal kingdom through the fable, for example. But one should beware of telling banal things to children, as is very often done, in the discussions during so-called "visual instruction." Above all, one should beware of presenting a fable by telling the story and then later adding all kinds of explanations, for everything you wish to accomplish through the telling will be destroyed by interpreting it. Children want to take in what is contained in a fable by feeling it. Children are terribly disturbed at a deep level, without being able to give an account of that fact, if they must listen after a story to banal explanations.

In the face of this knowledge, what might a person do who does not wish to get into the subtleties of the art of storytelling? That person might think: All right, I will leave out the explanations afterward and simply relate the fable. That is all well and good, but then children will not understand the fable and will certainly take no joy in it if it is not understood. If one wishes to speak Chinese to someone he or she must first teach the person Chinese, otherwise no correct understanding is gained of what one wishes to say in Chinese.

That is to say, it is also not correct to leave out the explanations. Instead of getting into explanations afterwards, one must try to give the explanations before telling the story. If you intend to tell a fable, such as "The Wolf and the Lamb," let us say, which we can also use to talk about the life of plants, you should first talk to the children about the wolf, its characteristics, and about the lamb, all oriented as much as possible to human beings. Try to put everything together in such a way that you feel the children really perceive the pictures and imagery that will then resonate in them when you tell them the story. If you include that which you would have offered in the form of an explanation afterward into a stimulating discussion prior to the story, then you do not destroy the sensation of feeling, but enliven it. If a child has already heard what a teacher is saying about the wolf and the lamb, then feelings become more active and lively and more joy is experienced in hearing the story.

Everything that must happen in the way of understanding must take place before the story is told. When they hear it, it must be brought to a height in the soul in order to understand it. So, one must conclude with telling a story and then do nothing else but let the sensations and feelings that have been stimulated in the children run their course. One must allow children to take their feelings and sensations home with them.

Creating the lessons so that everything is oriented toward human beings is important up until age 9. Those who have a sense for observing the transition that takes place around age 9 will recognize that this is the first time a child will be receptive to going out more into the natural world, albeit still from out of the human aspect. If one describes nature in and of itself, without relating it to human beings, children will not understand, even after age 9. You are deceiving yourself if you believe that the descriptions that are so often recommended in today's guidance on visual instruction will bring any kind of understanding to a child. Of course, one must begin natural history lessons after age 9, but one must always relate them to human beings. When teaching natural history one should not start with things in nature that are outside of human experience, but always start from the human aspect. One should always push the human being into the middle point and go out from there.

Let us assume that after age 9 we wish to help children understand the differences between the lower and higher animals and human beings. One begins with the human being: One compares both the lower and higher animals with some aspect of the human being. If one has described human beings in accordance with their physical characteristics, one can take what has been found in the human form and use that to compare with the lower and higher animals. Children understand this. One should not be concerned about over-reaching and speaking well beyond the subject of the animal world.

For example, let us say we take the opportunity to teach the children about a squid. First of all, one must have inner enthusiasm for the subject, and second, one must have a really good understanding of it. While always using the appropriate terms, one begins to demonstrate, e.g., To what part of the human being is a squid most related? Children can certainly understand that a squid is most related to the head of the human being. That is to say, in reality the lower animals are simply-formed, but the formations found in their simplicity recur in the form of the human head, only the human head is much more complex than in a lower animal. What is found with the higher animals, mammals, for instance, can be compared to what is found in the human torso. We must not compare higher animals to the life of the head in human beings, but only to the torso. When transitioning to the life of the limbs, we must say: "Look at the limbs of the human being. The way they are formed is just for people." The way human arms and hands are created as appendages to the body in which the soul-spiritual aspect can freely move—such a pair of limbs is not present in all of the animal kingdom. When one speaks of apes and their four hands, it is actually a misleading expression. Apes' limbs, by their very nature, are there to serve the purposes of holding things and moving the body. However, with human beings we see a remarkable differentiation between feet and hands, and arms and legs.

What is it that makes a human being human? It is not the head, is it? The head is just a more accomplished design of something that is already found in lower animals. That which is found in lower animals is further developed in the human head. But, the thing that makes a human being human, where human beings excel above the animal world, is the human limb system. Of course, what I have shown you here cannot be taught to children in this manner. You translate it so they slowly learn to perceive such things from this viewpoint. Then, through your teaching, you will do away with an endless amount that comes out of very mysterious substrata and spoils our present moral culture. In many instances our present moral culture is spoiled through the fact that people are endlessly prideful and arrogant about the head. However, they wouldn't feel that way if they were further informed about what basis underlies the human head system. On the other hand, they could be very proud of their limb system that serves for work and for placing oneself in the world of social order.

Lessons in natural science that are related to the animal world can, in an unconscious way, work into human nature in such a way that a right feeling for oneself and the social order is the result. This shows that questions of education have a much deeper foundation than is generally believed today, that they are connected with great, encompassing questions of culture. This sheds light on the teaching of natural science and how the lessons should be shaped after age 9. Everything is approached and treated as it relates to human beings, but in such a way that now, next to human beings, nature emerges everywhere and human beings appear to be a great aggregation, a centralization of nature. Children will gain a lot if this viewpoint is maintained until around age 12.

At approximately age 12, there is again an important notch in a child's development. At age 12, 13, or 14 (it varies with individuals) something plays into things that comes to expression after puberty: the ability to form opinions and make judgments. However, the ability to judge definitely plays into things in such a way that it must still work together with that which only comes out of the authority impulse. At this age, teachers must treat students in such a way that the impulse for authority and the power of judgment can work together in harmony. Thereupon the curriculum must be designed.

Then the time comes when we may start to teach natural history and, specifically, physical facts that are a complete departure from the human aspect, for example, refraction of light and the like. Children begin to understand the reverse process: applying nature to human beings. Up to age 12, through an inner impulse, children gain an understanding of nature by starting from the viewpoint of the human being, no longer in a moralizing way, but in the way I have just explained it. After age 12 children are ready to look at things that are detached and separate from human beings, but then to bring those things back and relate them to the human being. Children develop something that is never again lost to them if you, for instance, explain refraction through the lens of a camera and from there how this relates to refraction in the human eye, the whole inner structure of the eye. This is what you can teach children at this age.

A true curriculum develops out of knowledge of human beings at different ages. If we are really observant, children will reveal what they wish to learn at any given age. However, these are viewpoints that are not present in today's natural science. You simply will not arrive at these viewpoints, the immeasurable importance of the "Rubicon" that exists around age 9 and the second one around age 12, if you take in and present only the natural facts of any subject. These things must be produced from out of the whole nature of the human being—which includes body, soul, and spirit—while our mainstream natural science curriculum has limited itself to only the physical aspects of the human being.

One often hears discussions today about such things as whether one should look more to the formal, moral aspect in education, or see to it that a person develops according to predispositions and tendencies, or pay more attention to teaching such information as would be necessary for a later profession or occupation so that someone can fill a place in society. These questions appear childish when one understands the deeper basic principles from out of which human beings must be educated. External natural science does not recognize how an individual is connected with the whole of human evolution. But a supersensible perception of the history of human evolution does recognize this.

### GA 297, August 31, 1919, Page 73, Evening

One must be aware that beginning around age 9 comes a time when new, inner physical and mental forces appear in a person. If one introduces curriculum at this time that rightfully belongs only after age 12, one does harm to children, rather than good, and for the rest of their lives.

One must have sound knowledge of human life if one wishes to truly practice the art of education so that it is a service to human beings. One must understand how one should teach before and after age 9. It should not be that some old, ill-tempered school official is called upon to advise a department of education about the creation of a curriculum for whatever the outer concerns and considerations of the day may be—this for grade one, that for grade two, and so on. Nothing will come out of it that will help people confidently find their way in life. Human nature must teach us what we have to accomplish in education at each age level throughout childhood.

When you think about it, as adults, we are still learning from life. Life is our greatest teacher. But the possibility to learn from life does not exist until around age 15, 16, or 17 at the earliest. That is when we begin to stand before the world in such a way that we can learn from it. Until that time teachers in school are our world. We want to understand and love teachers as well as learn from them. Teachers should bring to us what is outside in the world. Between ages 7 and 15 there is a chasm between us and the world. Teachers must bridge that chasm.

## GA 297, September 8, 1920

Around age 9 children begin to differentiate from the world enough so that, from now on, we can begin to speak about plants and animals in a completely different way. In history lessons before that time we should proceed only pictorially, in the way of fairytales and legends. Out of this principal knowledge of human beings that we strive to achieve through spiritual science (not only in relation to general education and didactics) comes that which shows us what we must accomplish on a daily basis for the benefit of children's essential being; of the becoming human being. But all of this I have talked about still has a coating of thought and conceptualization attached to it. There is something else that is significantly more important.

Just think for a moment what it would mean for education if one took the following stance: In human beings we have standing before us simply the highest form of animal. We have to develop in human beings that which was received through physical birth. In contrast, through spiritual science, a teacher starts from this principle: A soul-spiritual being has descended from the spiritual world. This being is physically embodied as a human being. It has brought spiritual aspects with it from the spiritual world and joined with that which originated in the stream of heredity. We have this whole, living human mystery before us and we must work on this being's becoming. How one is overcome with an immense reverence for a becoming human being! What the gods in Heaven have sent to Earth is worthy of our awed reverence.

The second feeling that comes over us when we stand facing a child is an enormous sense of responsibility, albeit one that carries us and really gives us strength and will to teach. This is the thing that can enter into someone in a living way. I do not wish to be misunderstood; this is what I mean: That which enters into human beings as life, not theory or theoretical education or didactics, is the same thing that approaches us through spiritual science. Spiritual science does not only want to reflect the general world of life in its ideas; it encourages and allows human beings to participate in the general world of life. For this reason, educational activities stemming from spiritual science play a role that is really only first noticed when one becomes involved with and engages in the study of spiritual science.

### GA 297, December 29, 1920, Page 264

In the primary school years things are such that until about age 9 the majority of will activity is still tied to imitation. Then something happens within a child whereby he or she learns to differentiate from the environment. Anyone who is able to really observe children knows they are actually capable of rightly differentiating between subject and object, their own self and the environment, only beginning between ages 9 and 10 or thereabout. Everything we do must be based on this knowledge. There are probably many things in life we would look at differently or design differently if we recognized that during the life stages in which children learn to differentiate their own self from the environment, between ages 9 and 10, it is essential for their whole future moral life if they can, with the highest feelings of regard and acceptance of authority, depend on someone who is their teacher. If children cross this so-called Rubicon between ages 9 and 10 without these feelings, they will have a deficit for the rest of their lives. Only with the greatest effort can someone recapture in later life that which should have been imparted between ages 9 and 10.

As teachers we should make sure that in the class where children cross this Rubicon, between ages 9 and 10, we can stand before them in truth. Through our own inner sense of morality and truthfulness, the inner content of our soul, we can really be something to children, not simply a role model, but such that everything we say will be perceived as truth. One must originate and establish feelings in children which must exist in human social life between a maturing child and adults, including the elderly. A child's experiences of these feelings of reverence during this time between ages 9 and 10 are the basis for later moral-religious instruction.

The intellect should not be developed too early. One should take into consideration that which must be acted upon in the will through pictures and imagery from the beginning of primary school. One may not penetrate into the abstractions of reading and writing straight away. Such an understanding of the human being helps promote feelings and perceptions that are useful when we wish to teach about moral maxims, rules, and religious feelings. These things will not "take" later on, nor will they be accepted on authority, if we are not in a position to discern and utilize individual tendencies within the context of our knowledge of the whole human being beginning in primary school around age 7.

**GA 303, January 2, 1922, Page 319f.**

In answer to the fourth question: I think this question is answered with what I said in the first part of my lecture this morning. One cannot make a general statement that boys of this age go through a different crisis than the one I talked about this morning. It would be too much to assume that all boys in general become turbulent at this age. That is to say, if the transition I spoke about this morning is not guided by teachers in the right way, children (not just boys, but girls also) will in fact become very turbulent and disorderly. In a way they become restless and exhibit inner unwillingness, to the point it becomes difficult to get along with them. The thing that happens at this age is very different with each child depending on his or her temperament, but one must pay attention to it. Although generalizations do not really apply, this much one can say: If children are not guided properly in their entire development, to the point that they exhibit inner unwillingness, lacking an anchor, etc., and if the special turning point between ages 9 and 10 is not observed correctly by a teacher, the result will be as I have outlined above. This turning point must, under all circumstances, be noticed and observed by responsible teachers and educators.

**GA 304, November 23, 1921, Page 139f.**

If, because of me, as a teacher, a child of age 9 experiences this or that influence, how does that influence now appear in the underground of the whole etheric-soul life, and how might it later reappear? I give you the following concrete example: Through our educational methods we can instill in children of a tender age a feeling of exalted reverence and respect for what one encounters in the world. On the basis of this feeling, one can lead them into a religious sense, the sense through which children learn to pray.

I intentionally bring up this extreme example from out of children's moral condition. Let us assume we have correctly led a child to an inner place where he or she can let the soul flow out in an honest, simple prayer. This enters into a child's subconscious. Those who observe not merely someone's present condition of soul, but rather the whole organism of the soul and how it develops until death, will find that that which came to light in a child's prayerful reverence submerges and is transformed in the most varied ways in the soul life. At a certain age, perhaps at the beginning of the 30s or 40s, that which first appeared as prayerful devotion at a tender age now comes to light in the fact that the soul acquires the inner strength through which someone's words to others, especially children, have a quality of blessing.

That is how one studies the whole person relative to his or her soul development. Just as one relates the physical to the spatial, the stomach to the head, so one also relates that which appears as a force of prayer around age 8 or 9. If one is attentive over the course of a whole life, one sees it reappear as a power of blessing, a force that, in later life, also especially has a blessing effect on young people. Essentially, one can express it like this: No person in his or her 40s or 50s can have a blessing effect on those in the surroundings if he or she has not first learned to pray in an honest way as a child.

## Page 153ff.

There is one moment that is especially important and it occurs between ages 9 and 10, approximately in the middle of this seven-year epoch. It is a moment to which teachers and educators must pay especially close attention. Those who possess the ability to truly observe both the temporal and etheric organisms throughout a person's lifetime, as I have explained, know that in advanced age when a person is more inclined to contemplation and review of his or her earlier life, images appear in a person's mind, especially images of teachers and others who had a great influence on someone when they were between ages 9 and 10.

Such intimacies of life are unfortunately left completely unnoticed by today's researchers who are otherwise so exact with outwardly apparent things. The thing that happens with children between ages 9 and 10 (earlier or later depending on the individual) sinks into the subconscious. In later life it stands as an image before the soul, either joyfully or painfully, enlivening or deadening. This is a true observation and not a fantasy or a theory, and knowledge of it is immensely important for teachers. Directly at this age it becomes apparent that children need a teacher in such a way that a specific relationship can come to expression between a child and teacher.

As a teacher, if one simply pays attention to children, one will notice that around this age children ask an enormously important question of a teacher, more or less expressed, or perhaps withheld and unexpressed. And if, perhaps, a child is not inclined to openly ask the question, then a teacher must precipitate the circumstances in which the child can approach the teacher in a way that is appropriate at this age. What exactly is occurring?

Surely you do not expect the person who is speaking to you now, who also wrote *The Philosophy of Freedom* at the beginning of the 1890s, to suddenly advocate for authority out of some sense of conservative or reactionary principles. Simply from the perspective of the laws of child development alone, this must be emphasized: Just as up to the time of the change of teeth children are imitative beings, so it is that after the change of teeth their nature demands a kind of taken-for-granted, growing-into the authority of the environment as a condition of life. As a teacher, we must be able to exercise our self-evident authority with children. The reason they accept a truth must be because, in a loving way, they feel our authority. Children must lovingly feel this authority, not be forced into recognizing it. An enormous amount depends on this.

Again, one must have experience of these things. One must know what it means for the whole of a person's life relative to the configuration of his or her soul that someone experienced in childhood something like hearing others speak about a family member in an especially respectful way, as one would speak of a wise or good person or someone who is otherwise deserving of reverence. Then a child is brought before such a person and is in awe because the respect that has been implanted causes a child to look up to an authority figure with loving respect. Whoever has experienced something like this, has deepened his or her soul in this way when a child, knows that it made a permanent impression. It goes into the subconscious and comes to light again in later life. Something like this is the keynote that must resonate between a child and teacher.

From the change of teeth to puberty, children must absorb things through self-evident authority. Between ages 9 and 10, something happens within children that causes them to feel something that is sometimes very vague and undefined. It is a feeling that an authority figure has a connection with something higher. From out of the proximate, concrete relationship between a child and teacher, the child develops an interest in the spirituality of the teacher and where the teacher stands with respect to the supersensible universe.

## Page 156f.

It has to do not only with how we stand before a child with words, but also who we are and how we act around the children. This becomes especially important during the time indicated, between ages 9 and 10. I would like to paraphrase something that Goethe said: "Consider the way in which words are spoken and how they will be perceived. Are the words coming from an attitude of consciousness of an inner connection with the supersensible world or from a mind that is only materialistically inclined?" Between the ages of 9 and 10 a child should feel, completely unconsciously, that in the same way he or she looks up to a teacher and his or her authority, so the teacher in turn looks up to that which can no longer be seen externally. Of its own accord, the relationship between a child and teacher transitions from feelings for the human being into religious experience.

## GA 306, April 20, 1923

This is how it is with the awakening of love, except with a child it lasts for a period of approximately seven years. Love comes alive with everything we approach children with in a likeable manner when we begin to teach the first subjects in school. If we begin with this pictorial approach as I have already described it, we will see love coming to meet us from out of this activity. Everything must be bathed in love. If one makes a comparison with normal waking activity, children are actually still deep inside their sleeping, or dreaming, consciousness. This softens the blow of a stronger jolt into a waking life of consciousness. Through all of that which I described yesterday and the day before about the time between ages 9 and 10, and then especially around age 12, children's love of nature awakens. That is when we will notice it for the first time.

Before this time, children display a completely different attitude toward nature: love for everything fairylike that enlivens nature, which must be pictorially created when we interact with them. Then, love for the realities of nature awakens. Here we have a particularly difficult task in handling things that fall into this phase—causality, how to approach things that are not alive, the approach to historical connections, beginning with the laws of physics and chemistry. As teachers we have the great task of bringing grace into all of this.

I am not joking. I say this in all earnestness. It is absolutely necessary that we bring true grace into our teaching of geometry and physics, for example. Our teaching must become gracious and, above all, we may not be acerbic or peevish. That is exactly where education in these subjects suffers so much between the ages of 11½ or 11¾ and 14 or 15. It seems these subjects are often taught with a sour disposition, when the things that must be taught about light refraction, light reflection, calculating the area of a sphere, etc., are brought up not with an attitude of grace, but with peevishness.

## GA 308, April 8, 1924, Page 11f.

Indeed one thing must be taken into consideration: Knowledge of the human being, especially the becoming human being, a child, is all too often regarded in such a way that we think of having a child for only a certain period of time. We concentrate our efforts. We ask questions about developmental forces, questions like: How do these forces work at a given age and what should we do to meet these developmental forces in the right way at any given age? However, knowledge of human beings the way it is meant here has to do with not only these particular, unique moments of experience; such knowledge has to do with a person's entire earthly life. This is not as easy to observe as a narrowly defined period of time in someone's life. However, for teachers, it is necessary to consider the whole of a person's life on Earth because the seeds we plant in a child at age 8 or 9 have their effects when that child becomes an adult of 45 or 50 years old.

As teachers, the things we do and say during the school years go deep into a person's physical, psychical, and spiritual nature. They weave their way under the surface, often for decades, and then, in a remarkable way, sometimes even at the end of a person's life, that which was planted as a seed at the beginning of life comes to light. One can act upon a child's nature in the right way only if one considers not only the childhood years, but also the whole of a person's life in the light of true knowledge of the human being.

I have in mind such knowledge when I now present you with individual examples, merely as indications, of how the soul of a teacher can intimately affect the soul of a child. We will understand what we should do regarding a child's schooling, his or her intellectual schooling and guidance for will impulses, only if we first understand what is active between a teacher and a child, just by the fact that teachers and children are there, each with their own particular nature, temperament, character, level of education, and a very unique physical and mental constitution. Before we ever begin to teach, we and the children are simply there. There is already impact and effect between us. How teachers act toward children is the first significant question.

**GA 310, July 22, 1924, Page 107ff.**

One needs parents' cooperation so that nothing hinders a child's acceptance of a teacher's self-evident authority, which must be present. A lot of work must be done to forge paths of understanding between teachers and parents. Some parents are jealous of their child's teacher. They may feel that a teacher wants to take their child away, in a manner of speaking. As soon as this attitude is present there is not much more that can be done with a child in an educational sense. But this situation can be remedied if a teacher understands immediately that support must be garnered from parents. By getting to know a teacher well, parents should be able to overcome any feelings of jealously they might have. This is something I must add to what I have already said about what the weekly teacher's conferences should include.

What we are really concerned with is trying to understand all the moments in a child's life that are significant transitions. I have already mentioned one such time period in which the previous fairytale-like pictorial quality of the lessons must transition into teaching about plant life, for example. This time period is between ages 9 and 10. A child displays something akin to inner restlessness. All kinds of feelings come to the forefront that prompt the question: What is happening with this child? He or she does not know what is going on, but there is an inner feeling of restlessness and all kinds of questions are asked. The content of the questions is usually of no great significance, but the very fact that a child is asking, that questions even come up, is indeed significant.

At this point in time, what one does with a child in terms of the relationship between teacher and child holds great significance for a child's whole life. What is it that is within a child? It is within every child, as long as there is nothing pathologically wrong. Until now, unless someone has been ruined by outside influences, he or she has accepted the natural authority of a teacher as a matter of course. A healthy child also has a quite healthy respect for every adult unless he or she has been previously told all manner of things that would spoil those feelings of respect. Just think back to your own childhood and what it means, especially for someone very young, if a child is able to think: 'You may do what he does or what she does. He or she is a good and worthy person.' A child really has no other desire than to be placed under authority.

In a certain sense, this desire is somewhat shaken between the ages of 9 and 10, simply through the development of human nature itself. One must be able to understand this completely. The nature of a human being arrives at this time period for the purpose of feeling something very specific. It does not rise into a child's consciousness, but lives in undefined feelings and perceptions. Children also cannot express it, but it is there. What is a child unconsciously saying? Before this time period a child's perceptions are: That which the teacher says is good is indeed good, and that which the teacher says is bad is indeed bad. Something is wrong because the teacher says it is wrong. Something is beautiful because the teacher finds it so, and something is ugly because the teacher finds it ugly. For a child, a teacher is the absolutely accepted norm. During the time period between ages 9 and 10, this inner acceptance is somewhat shaken. Feelings arise in children that prompt them to ask: Where does the teacher get all of this? Who is the authority for the teacher? Where is this authority?

From this moment there begins to be an inner urge within a child to break through the visible aspect of the person that has up to now been like a god to the child, to break through to the supersensible or invisible god or divinity that stands behind the being of the authority figure. One must simply prove this to a child somehow. One must stand before a child in such a way that he or she feels the teacher is supported, in a supersensible sense, that the teacher does not speak arbitrarily from his or her own nature, but is like a missionary for the divine aspect in the supersensible world.

This is the feeling one must instill in a child. But how? Lecturing is the very least effective way. One can talk about it, of course, but one accomplishes the least through lecturing. Rather, one can approach a child, and perhaps say something the subject of which is of no particular significance, but which is spoken in such a way that a child understands that this person has a heart and that heart believes in what stands invisibly behind him or her. One can really accomplish something with this approach. In the right way, a child's attention must be directed to how a teacher stands within the world.

Children are already wise enough, although not in an abstract, rational sense, that they come and ask: "Oh, I would like to know…?" Children come with such questions at this age. You could answer something like this, for example: "That which I can give to you I receive from the Sun. If the Sun weren't there, I would not be able to give you anything in this life. When we sleep the Moon keeps everything that we get from the Sun during the day. So, if the Moon weren't there, I also would not be able to give you anything." This does not yet hold much meaning for children, but if it is said with such warmth that they understand you love the Sun and Moon, you will satisfy them and lead them up and over these questions, usually for their lifetime.

One must understand that these crisis-like moments are present in children's lives. Then you will have the feeling that until now you have depended upon the spruce and the oak, the buttercup and the dandelion, the sunflower and the violet, and all manner of fairytale-like beings to help you tell the children about nature, thereby leading them into a spirit-filled world. But now the time has come when one can begin to tell stories from the Gospels. If one begins earlier than now, or with some catechism-like instruction, then one destroys something in children. But if one begins with it now, when they are just beginning to penetrate into the spiritual world, then one has done something for which their whole being is longing.

**GA 311, August 12, 1924, Page 13**

Let us assume I have a pale child sitting in the classroom. A pale child should appear to me as a puzzle that I have to solve. Many causes are possible, but let us say the case is as follows: The child started school with rosy cheeks and has become pale while in my class. I admit this, but now I must figure out why the child has become pale. Perhaps I will come to the idea that I gave him or her too much learning material that overburdened the memory. If I do not acquiesce, if I am a shortsighted pedagogue and have imagined that a method must be carried out to completion regardless of whether a child becomes flushed or pale thereby, then the child will remain pale.

Then if I were somehow in a position to observe this child when he or she is 50 years old, this person would probably suffer from a terrible sclerosis, would have arteriosclerosis and not understand from where it came. It came from the fact that I overburdened the memory when the child was 8 or 9 years old. Yes, you see, the 50-year-old and the 8- or 9-year-old belong together; this is, after all, a human being. We must understand what the result is of something we did with a child after 40 or 50 years have passed, because life is a unified whole. All life stages are connected. Merely to know a child is not enough; we must know about the whole human being at all stages of life.

### GA 311, August 13, 1924, Page 30

Much depends on one being acutely aware of how children transition into the life of imagination at the age that includes the change of teeth. They do not transition into the life of intellect, but of imagination. As a teacher you must be able to facilitate this development. Development of the life of imagination can be facilitated by people in whose souls is a true knowledge of the human being. It is true that knowledge of the human being allows the inner soul life to thaw, so to speak, allows for a smile to become part of the physiognomy of the face. A grouchy, morose disposition comes from a lack of knowledge.

Of course, it is certainly possible that someone has an illness from an improperly functioning organ and thus facial expressions may reflect that illness. But that sort of thing does not bother children; they look past that. However, what from the innermost part of the soul is expressed in the physiognomy and is filled with knowledge of the human being is what makes a teacher capable of becoming a true educator.

Between the time of the change of teeth and puberty, education must take place within the realm of imagination. I would say that what is present in a child in the first few years is completely sense organ in nature, and it then becomes more internalized and more mental in nature. Sense organs, of course, do not think. They perceive images, or, more precisely, they create images from external things. Even though that which a child develops as a sense organ becomes more mental in nature, it still produces no thought, but rather an image, albeit a mental image, an imagination. For this reason one must work with children through the use of pictures and imagery.

The least effective way of working pictorially with children is if, from the outset, one approaches them with something completely foreign. One example is what we have today in our writing, whether handwritten or printed, it makes no difference. Children can absolutely not relate to something like the letter "A." And why should they have a relationship to something like an "A"? Why should children in any way be interested in the letter "L"? The letters of the alphabet are something completely foreign to children. In spite of this fact, when they enter school these things are taught. The result is that children feel completely alienated from that which is supposed to be achieved. And if one goes so far as to approach them with these things before the change of teeth, allowing their mind to be stuffed full of all kinds of cut-out forms of alphabet letters, you are encouraging children to be concerned with things that are very far removed from them, and to which they have not the least ability to relate.

In contrast, at the outset children possess an artistic sense and imagination. One must appeal to this artistic, imaginative sense; this is where one must turn. One must absolutely not try to approach them with conventional letters of the alphabet that are a product of human civilization. One must try to go through the cultural development of humanity in a sage and spirit-filled way, if you will forgive me the use of that term.

## Page 31

Consider the following: Let us take the word "mouth," for example. Have the children draw a mouth and let them do it using a paintbrush and dabs of red color and then have them pronounce the word "mouth." Next, have them say only the beginning "M" sound. The painting can be gradually formed so that the upper lip becomes the letter "M." In this way we can get the letter "M" from out of the mouth that was painted. This is really the way writing came about, only today it is difficult to discern that the letters were actually pictures because during the course of language development, the words were shifted and became displaced. Originally, every sound had its corresponding picture that was distinct and unmistakable.

## Page 37ff.

The underpinning of all classroom lessons should be the quality of imagination. One must clearly understand that before age 9 or 10 children do not know how to differentiate their "I" from the environment. They have long spoken using the "I" form only by instinct. But, in reality, children actually feel themselves to be within, and part of, the whole world. They feel related to the whole world. Today, relative to this, there exist quite adventurous ideas. It is said of primitive tribes that their perception of the world is defined by animism and that they treat lifeless objects as if those objects had an enlivened soul. And, one is convinced of one's own understanding of children when it is said that they behave in their realm exactly like primitive tribes, for if a child bumps into an object with sharp corners, the child will hit the object because it is accounted as possessing a soul, as being alive.

But this is absolutely not true. In reality, children do not ensoul objects, but rather they cannot yet differentiate between living things and lifeless objects. Children look at everything as a unity and see themselves as unified with the surroundings. Beginning between ages 9 and 10, children learn to actually differentiate the environment. One must strictly take this into consideration if one wishes to tactically plan the whole curriculum. It is important that one refers to plants, animals, even rocks, as if these things talk to one another, behave with each other like people, tell each other things, and hate and love each other. One must use anthropomorphism in the most inventive ways and treat everything as if it were human. But do not ensoul things in a livening sense, but rather handle things in a way that is oriented toward children's understanding, realizing they cannot yet differentiate between lifeless objects and living things. There is not yet any reason for children to think that a rock has no enlivening soul but a dog does. No, although children begin to differentiate the two by seeing that a dog moves and a rock does not, they do not attribute movement to an enlivening soul.

What it comes down to is that one is able to treat all living things as if they are people talking together, thinking, and feeling, just as if they are people who develop sympathies and antipathies toward one another. Therefore, everything that one brings to children at this age must be in the manner of fairytales and legends. Through this they receive the very, very best disposition of soul for their instinctive, imagination-filled soul-nature.

During this time if children are filled up with all kinds of intellectual things (and that will happen if everything that one teaches is not translated into pictorial imagery), later they will feel the effects in the blood vessels and circulatory system. I must repeat, again and again, a child's entire life must be viewed as a unified whole. In order to do this, a teacher must have a sense of artistry in his or her soul, be inclined to the artistic, because that which a teacher effects in a child is not merely what one can devise, or concepts one can teach, but rather it is, if I may use the expression, the imponderables of life. An enormous amount is transferred from teacher to child unconsciously. A teacher must be aware of this when telling stories, fairytales, and legends. Very, very often, in our materialistic times, it happens that teachers look upon these stories as childish and something they do not really believe. Here, you see, anthroposophy appears really in the right way when it is the guide to true knowledge of the human being. Through anthroposophy we are aware that one can express something with much more richness if it is clothed in imagery than if it is expressed through the use of abstract concepts and terms. Healthy children have a need for everything to be brought to them pictorially, and also to receive that imagery into their being.

**Page 40f.**

There is something extraordinarily significant that happens when children are between ages 9 and 10. Teachers must make note of it. Abstractly speaking, between ages 9 and 10 children learn to differentiate from the environment. They perceive their own self as "I" and the surroundings as something on the outside that does not belong to the "I." But this is the abstract explanation. The reality is closer to the fact that at this age children approach a beloved teacher with some kind of difficulty. In most cases they do not articulate what is really bothering them.

One must understand that this is coming out of the substrata of the soul. One must find the right answer, attitude, and behavior. Very much depends upon this for the rest of a person's life. You can teach and work with children of this age only if you are a natural authority figure and they have the feeling something is true because you think it is true, something is beautiful because you point out its beauty, and something is good because you say it is good. You must be the representative of all that is good, true, and beautiful. Children must be drawn to truth, beauty, and goodness because they are drawn to you.

Between ages 9 and 10, a feeling comes over a child, very instinctively in his or her subconscious: "I learn everything from my teacher, but where does this knowledge originate? What is it that stands behind my teacher?" There is no need to remark further about this. If one gets into explanations or definitions, it does only harm. But the important thing is that one finds the right words that are heartfelt and infused with warmth. Whatever it is that is troubling a child usually lasts for a period of weeks or months. The crisis within a child involves the principle of authority. If one is up to the task and understands to put much heart and soul into the way one meets the challenges at this point in time by approaching a child with the needed inwardness, credibility, and truthfulness so as to preserve one's authority, that child will not waver in belief in people's goodness. One has thereby also maintained the child's acceptance of a teacher's natural authority which is, of course, good for one's continued teaching. But it is in the nature of human beings that between the ages of 9 and 10 they may not be put off from their confidence in good people; otherwise all feelings of inner security that should be a guide for future life will be called into question as well.

This is extremely important and we must take heed of such things. It is much more important than all the tiny little things that are prescribed in education today. We must understand what happens at specific times in children's lives and how we should act so the light of our behavior will shine forth for the rest of their lives.

# Teaching Content for the Ninth Year of Life

**GA 294, August 28, 1919, Page 95ff.**

You will have to make do with many simpler means for which normal public or state-funded schools have abundant resources. That may, indeed, make your teaching livelier, but it could also make the teaching of some subjects quite bitter for you. You will feel this particularly when you have brought the children to the end of their ninth year and can really only continue teaching if there are adequate resources and materials available. You will then have to use drawing and simple, elementary painting as a substitute for some things which, in ideal conditions, you would not convey by drawing or painting, but by a study of the object itself. I have made these preliminary remarks because today I would like to speak to you about the transition relative to didactics [method] which must be attended to as soon as the children have passed their ninth year. We will understand the curriculum during this time period only if we have further instructed ourselves in method to the point that we recognize and comprehend the essential nature of each individual child between ages 7 and 15. I would like to demonstrate what, as teachers, you will have to make clear to children in this respect (in a rather different, more basic way), right when they are between ages 9 and 10. With some children, this point is reached already before age 9, and with some it happens later, but on average that which I will tell you about today begins at age 9.

When we approach this time period, we must sense the necessity of also introducing natural history subjects into the lesson plan. Before this time, natural history subjects were brought to the children as narratives, in story form, just as I said yesterday in the seminar on the human being's relationship to the animal and plant kingdoms.*

---

*See #3 of Volume 6 of the periodical, *The Art of Education* –tr.

Before, one will bring natural history subjects to the children in more of a descriptive, storytelling form. However, you will not have actually begun with real teaching of natural history until the Rubicon of age 9/10 has been crossed.

It is now of great importance to understand that what should be effected in children by natural history lessons is thoroughly spoiled if one does not begin the lessons by grappling with and dealing with the subject of the human being. You may say, justifiably: "When a child is 9 years old, one will be able to tell them a little about the natural history of humankind." It may be ever so little, but the little bit one can teach children about humankind one brings as a preparation for all other natural history lessons.

As you do this, you will need to know that, in a manner of speaking, there is a synthesis within the human being. There exists an aggregation of all three kingdoms of nature in the human being whereby the three natural kingdoms are combined at a higher level. You will not need to tell children about this, but through the course of the lessons you must promote a feeling that the human being is a compendium of all the other kingdoms of nature. You will accomplish this if you give the discussions about humankind the necessary emphasis and if the way you deal with the subject of humankind prompts the impression in children that human beings are very important within the whole natural world order.

When children are around 9 years old, you will perhaps begin to describe the external aspects of the human form. You will call their attention to the main structural organization of the human being consisting of head, torso, and limbs, but in doing so you will give more consideration to outward appearance, the outer form. It would be good if you have already elicited a concept of the main aspects of the human form through the aid of previous, well-kept drawings in which the head is round, somewhat flattened on the underside, and rests on the torso at this flattened spot. That is to say, the head is like a ball sitting on top of the torso of the body. It is good to call forth this image. It simultaneously awakens feeling and will elements because children begin by looking at the head from an artistic standpoint, from its round form.

This is important. In this way you capture the whole person, not just the intellect. Then you try to bring about the notion that the torso is, in a manner of speaking, a fragment of the head. Try to bring this about through a drawing, whereby you say: "The head has a round shape." Remove a portion of the sphere by cutting it away so, in a manner of speaking, the Moon remains behind from the Sun; that is how you get the main shape of the torso. It would be good to shape a ball out of wax or kneaded dough, cut out a portion and leave the Moon behind as a truly round form so the children get a true understanding of the idea that the human torso is formed from a fragment of the sphere. For the limbs you awaken the idea that they are appended to the torso and affixed to it. There is much that children will not be able to understand, but at least call up a vivid picture that the limbs are "fixed into" the human organism. At this point you must not go any further, for the limbs are continued internally in the morphological constitution of the human being, and are there connected with the digestive and sexual organs, which are simply a continuation of the limbs in an inward direction. But you evoke the clear idea that the limbs are affixed to the organism from outside. This gives children an initial concept of the human form.

Try to elicit an initial, though still elementary, concept that our round head enables us to view the world. One can say: "You have your eyes, ears, nose, and mouth in your head. You see with your eyes, hear with your ears, smell with your nose, and taste with your mouth. Most of what you know about the outside world is because of your head." If you develop these thoughts further, children develop an understanding of the special formation and function of the head. Then you try to create a concept of the torso by telling them: "What you taste with your tongue goes into your torso as food and what you hear with your ears goes into your torso as sound."

It is good to give children an idea of the system of organs in the whole human being by pointing out that the chest organs allow one to breathe and the abdominal organs allow one to digest food. Furthermore, it is good to let them reflect on how human limbs have feet on one end that serve for walking and running, and on the other end are hands that move freely and help us to work. It is good if, already as a child, one is given to understand the difference between the services rendered to a human body by feet and hands. Our feet carry us and make it possible to work at all the varied places we live. In contrast, our arms and hands must not carry us, but they allow us to work freely. While our legs and feet help us stand on the ground, our arms and hands can be extended in the air to help us work. In short, the essential difference between human legs and feet, and human arms and hands, should be pointed out early on. The difference between the service provided by feet and legs in carrying the body and that provided by arms and hands in that they do not only serve the human body, but also work for the world—this difference between the egoistic service of feet and the unselfish service of hands in working for the outside world of humanity should be sensitively taught to children early on.

We work out the concept from out of the form and in this way we should teach as much as possible about human beings from a natural history perspective. Only then does one get into the rest of natural history, starting with the animal kingdom. Here it would be good if you could figure out some way to bring a squid and a mouse, a lamb, or even a horse to the class, something from this group of mammals, and then perhaps again a representation of the human being, of which you should have plenty on hand since you only need to have a student act as your human example.

You must be very clear in your mind about how you will proceed. First, you will introduce the squid and try to familiarize the students with it. You will tell them how the squid lives in the sea and, through observation or drawing, you will describe how it looks.

When you describe a squid, children will feel you are describing it in a very particular way. Perhaps only later, when you describe a mouse, for instance, will they notice how differently you describe the mouse than the squid. You must try to develop this aesthetic by the way you go about describing a squid in a different way than a mouse while at the same time prompting the children to get a feeling for the differences between these two animals. With the squid, you must emphasize how it feels something of what is in its surroundings. If a squid senses anything dangerous nearby, it immediately puts out some of its dark, inky liquid and surrounds itself with an inky aura to deter predators. One can tell the children many things which will help them understand that when a squid acts, when it defends itself against predators in any way, or when it feeds, it is always acting the same way a person acts when he or she looks at something or eats something, for example. When a human being eats something he experiences a "taste," a feeling, which comes to him by way of the tongue, the organ of taste. And, a human eye continually has a need to look at light. By doing this, the eye is able to come to grips with light and explain it, in a manner of speaking. Because of the fact that their taste organs desire the experience of taste, human beings eat food.

Describe a squid in such a way that children can feel the sensitivity of the squid to the environment with its finely-tuned perception of its surroundings. You will have to work out an artful description of a squid so the children can really grasp the subject through your artistry of presentation.

Then you come to the description of a mouse. You will describe how a mouse has a pointy nose and that the first things you notice about its nose are the whiskers growing on either side of it. The other very noticeable thing about a mouse is its upper and lower incisor teeth, its gnawing teeth. Next describe a mouse's disproportionately large ears, cylindrical shaped body, and very soft, velvety hair. Talk about its limbs, the little forefeet and somewhat larger hind feet which enable a mouse to jump very well. Then there is the scaly tail with very little hair on it. Notice how the mouse supports itself on its tail when it wants to hold something in its forepaws or climb. Because a mouse's tail is covered with scales instead of hair, a mouse has much more inner sensitivity to anything touching its tail, which makes it very useful. In short, as before, you will try to describe a mouse in such a way that its form is artfully constructed. This can be accomplished if you evoke the idea that a squid does not need appendages growing out of its body in the same way as a mouse. A squid's body has enough sensitivity on its own. It does not need big ears like a mouse. A squid stands in such a relationship to the environment that it can bring food into itself without needing a pointy nose like a mouse. A squid also does not need such large, attached limbs like a mouse because it can use its body to propel itself forward in the water. A squid expresses itself less through its limb system and more through its body. Summarize correctly what you teach in an artistic way.

I must describe everything to you first so that you can translate it into your lessons. You must be consciously aware of what you will later more unconsciously bring into artistically created lessons. In short, describe a mouse in such a way that the children gradually get the feeling that a mouse is made so that its limb system is completely in service to the life of its torso. Then clearly explain that lambs are also made that way and horses too. If a horse lives in the wild, the life of its torso is served by its limbs. For example, explain the following: Look at a mouse. It has really sharp, pointed teeth. Its teeth have to be sharp and pointed; otherwise it could not gnaw through things as it must to feed itself and burrow holes in which to live. By doing this its teeth are continually worn down. However, a mouse is made so that its teeth, like our fingernails and toenails, keep on growing from the inside so it always has a replacement for the substance of its teeth that gets worn away. One sees, especially with the teeth, which are also organs that are appended to the rest of the body, that they are designed to enable the torso-body of a mouse to live.

In this way you give children a strong, albeit rudimentary, impression of a squid in accordance with the feeling-nature. Furthermore, you awaken a strong impression about the physical structure of a mouse. Now, you will once again turn to the physical structure of the human being. If we look for that part of the human being that has the most in common with a squid, we are drawn to the human head, curiously enough. The part of a person that most resembles a squid is the head. It is biased preconception that makes people think of the head as the most perfect body part. Of course, the head has a very complicated structure but, essentially, it is only a transformed squid. What I mean to say is that the human head is a transformed lower animal because it relates to the environment in a similar way. With the torso, the human being is most similar to higher animals, such as a mouse, lamb, or horse. While a squid is able to stay alive with only its head, a human being cannot do this. The human head must be placed on the torso and rest there. It cannot move about freely. A squid, which is basically only a head and nothing else, can move freely about in the water. You must emphasize this in such a way as to give the impression that lower animals are simply heads that can move about freely, but they are not as perfected as the human head. And, you must awaken a feeling that higher animals are mainly torsos and that nature has expertly formed their organs and appendages mainly for the purpose of satisfying the needs of their torso. It is less so with human beings. Where their torso is concerned, human beings are less perfectly formed than higher animals.

One must bring children to the point of feeling that there is a feature of the outer human form that is the most perfected of all species, and that is the human limb system. If you look at all the higher animals, up to the apes, you will find their front limbs are not so very different from their back limbs and, for all intents and purposes, their limbs serve only to carry their torso and propel it forward, etc. This wonderful differentiation of the limbs into feet and hands and arms and legs first appears in human beings, and their development is pronounced in the human being's predisposition to an upright gait and posture. In respect to the coordination and organization of the limb system, no animal species is so perfectly formed as human beings.

Next, one introduces a quite visual description of human arms and hands, how they have been relieved of the task of carrying the body and how hands do not come in contact with the earth in service. Then one transitions into the moral-will aspect. For example, oriented toward the feeling-nature, without being theoretical, one gives children this vivid impression: Take a piece of chalk in your hand to write on the blackboard. You can do this only because your hand has been transformed into something able to perform tasks and is no longer needed to carry the body. Talking about arms, one cannot say that animals are lazy because, basically, animals do not have arms. If one speaks about apes as having four hands that is only an imprecise figure of speech because in reality apes have four arm-like legs and feet, not four hands. Of course, these animals are made to climb, but even climbing is something that serves the body. Their feet have a hand-like form so they can support their body when climbing. In terms of supporting the body, human arms and hands are without purpose which is what makes them the most wonderful outward representation of human freedom! There exists no more beautiful symbol of human freedom than arms and hands. Through the use of hands, human beings can work for the good of the environment and others around them, and because they eat food they can also support their own body through the work of their hands by their own free will.

This is how, through the descriptions of a squid, mouse, lamb, or horse, and the human being one awakens in children, through their feeling-nature, a strong perception that lower animals are characterized by the head, higher animals by the torso, and the human being by the limbs.

It only leads to engendered arrogance if one always teaches that the human being is the most perfected living thing on Earth because of the head. Through this kind of teaching, someone will involuntarily absorb the idea that one is perfected through laziness and inactivity because, instinctively, a person knows that the head is a lazybones and sits on the shoulders and rests. It does not wish to move itself through the world but is carried by the limbs. It is not true that the human being is the most perfected living thing through the head, the lazy head, but rather through the limbs which are integrated into the world and work in it. You help make someone more of a moral person when you do not teach that humans are perfectly complete because of a slothful head, but rather because of active limbs. The creatures that are only head, like the lower animals, must move the head themselves, and creatures which use their limbs only in service to the torso, like the higher animals, are less perfect creatures when compared to human beings because higher animals are less able to freely use their limbs than are human beings. An animal's limbs are already constrained by a certain purpose. They serve the torso at all times.

With the human being, one pair of limbs, the hands, is completely released into the sphere of human freedom. You can teach someone to have a healthy perception of the world only if you awaken the idea that they are perfectly complete because of the limbs, not the head. This can be accomplished easily through comparative descriptions of a squid, mouse, lamb, or horse, and a human being. At the same time, you will also notice that there is never a time, while describing anything in nature, that the human being should not be brought into it because all the activities of nature are united in the human being. That is why we should always have the human being in the background when we describe anything in nature. Also for this reason, when children have reached age 9 and we begin lessons in natural history, the human being should be our starting point.

Those who observe children will discover that something happens between ages 9 and 10. It is not as clearly apparent as the first bump in the process that occurs at an earlier age. When children begin to move their limbs a little more consciously and often even walk a little awkwardly, when they begin to move their arms and hands purposefully, it is the approximate time when children begin to become conscious of the "I." Later they will be able to remember back to this point in time, but nothing earlier. When you notice children beginning to say "I" at the indicated age, or perhaps even a little later since the activity of speech, the will element, must be developed first, you can see that their initial consciousness of self is very clearly discernible at this age whereas it is not so easily discerned with the changes surrounding the consciousness of self that occur around age 9. Around age 9 children's consciousness of self is strengthened. One notices they have a much better grasp of things learned about the differences between the human being and the world.

Before the Rubicon of the ninth year, children are "fused" with the environment to a much greater extent than after they have reached this age. Afterward, children differentiate much more from the environment. For this reason one can now begin to talk a little about things of the soul and children will not appear to lack understanding as much as they did before age 9. In short, the consciousness of self is deepened and strengthened when they reach age 9.

Those who have a sense for such things will notice that children of this age begin to use words much more inwardly. They become more aware that words originate from within a person. Today, when people seem to be more concerned with external rather than internal things, there is much too little attention given to this transition around age 9 to 10. But teachers must direct their attention to this transitional period. Thus, your prevailing tone will be completely different during lessons in natural history, which must always compare the human being to the other kingdoms of nature after this point in time. Whereas before, when children were more grown together with nature, one could only talk about natural science in the form of stories, now, after age 9, we can begin to present a squid, mouse, lamb, or horse, along with the human being and animals' relationships to the human form.

Before this age you would have touched on something that is incomprehensible to children if you tried to make the connection between a squid and a human head, or if you tried to relate a mouse to a human torso, or searched for the thing that lifts the human being above all the other natural kingdoms in the human limb system. Children come toward you and offer something at this special age. You should make use of what they bring for the simple reason that if you make use of the indications I have provided for teaching natural science, you will have brought very solid, unwavering moral concepts into children's souls.

One does not bring moral concepts into the soul by appealing to the intellect, but rather by appealing to the feeling- and will-natures. One does this by directing children's thoughts and feelings to the notion that people are fully human only when they use their hands to perform tasks for the world, and how, by working with their hands, they are the most complete, and that there is a relationship between the human head and a squid, the human torso and a mouse, sheep, or horse. Through these feelings of being placed into the natural order of things, children also absorb feelings through which they will later understand that they are truly human.

You can impart this especially important moral element into a child's soul if you make an effort to create natural history lessons so a child does not suspect that you wish to teach morals. However, you will never teach even a hint of morality if you teach natural history as something separate from the human being by describing a squid, mouse, lamb and horse as separate, independent creatures, or even describing the human being that way. Such an approach would involve nothing more than verbal definitions. The human being may be described only as related to all other organisms, creatures, and activities in nature.

Schiller admired Goethe for his naïve concept of nature which consisted of thinking of the human being as put together from all of the individual parts of nature; this idea was expressed in a wonderful letter that Schiller wrote to Goethe at the beginning of the 1790s. I have brought up this letter time and again because it contains something that, ideally, should completely cross over into our culture, that is, consciousness of the synthesis of the whole of nature in the human being.

Goethe expressed it like this: "Human beings have been placed at the pinnacle of nature and there they feel as if they are a whole nature unto themselves." He also said it like this: "Within the human being the whole rest of the world actually comes into its consciousness." If you go through my writings, you will find such sayings by Goethe quoted again and again. I did not quote them simply because I like them but because such ideas need to cross over into our *Zeitgeist*, into the consciousness of our time. That is why I am always so grieved that one of the most significant written works on education is pretty much completely unknown, or at least has remained unfruitful within the actual institutions of education.

Schiller learned sound educational theory from Goethe's naïve self-education, and he incorporated what he learned into his work titled "Briefe über die aesthetische Erziehung des Menschen" ("Letters on the Aesthetic Education of Man"). These letters contain a tremendous amount of sound educational theory. One must only think beyond them and consequentially think through what they contain. It is certain that Schiller arrived at his theories by way of the opinions and views of Goethe. Just think how Goethe, a product of his civilization but simultaneously rooted in nature, from earliest childhood, opposed the educational principles of his era. Goethe could never separate the human being from the environment. He always thought of the human being in the context of nature and felt himself, as a human being, to be one with nature. That is why, for instance, he did not enjoy piano lessons as long as they were given in such a way as to be completely isolated from nature in human beings. He became interested in piano lessons only when he was shown the function of each individual finger, when he heard: "This is the thumb and this is the index finger," etc., and understood how they could be used to play the piano. He always wanted to have the whole human being standing in the midst of the whole of nature.

And something else, which I have mentioned before: When Goethe was 7 years old, he built himself a nature altar. He took a music stand that belonged to his father and plants and rocks from his father's herbarium to arrange around the stand. He put an incense candle on top and caught the rays of the morning sun in a burning glass as an offering to the great god of nature, a rebellion against that which his educational upbringing wished to teach him. Goethe always lived his life as a person who *wanted* to be educated as someone in our newer age *should* be educated. Schiller admired him so much because he was that way, struggling with himself to become who he was. And then Schiller wrote about education in his "Aesthetic Letters," the content of which we are aware.

## GA 294, August 29, 1919, Page 111

Finding the right curriculum for the time between ages 7 and 14–15 is generally linked to a real knowledge of child development. Yesterday we highlighted a developmental moment that occurs between ages 9 and 10. When we follow child development from age 7 through to ages 8 and 9, before age 10 is reached we have a point somewhere around that time that I have characterized by the following: The "I"-consciousness is strengthened and consolidated so that from this time onward we can approach a child with concepts of natural history in the way I told you about yesterday with a squid and mouse, lamb, or horse, and the human being. You will understand that in doing so, you should still always take into consideration the interactive relationship of the human being and the environment, how the human being is actually an aggregation of all the rest of the kingdoms of nature and how they cannot yet be sharply delineated from the rest of nature. One spoils an enormous amount for a becoming person if one does not proceed in such a way that a child of 10 or 11 is always guided, through feelings and perceptions, to the idea of how the human being is connected with external nature and is a synthesis of the external natural world.

However, there is another important point in child development between ages 12 and 13. At this time a person's soul-spiritual aspect is strengthened and energized insofar as this soul-spiritual aspect is less dependent upon the "I." What is referred to in spiritual science as the astral body vitalizes and joins itself with the etheric body. Of course, the astral body is only truly born as an independent body at puberty, but through the etheric body, it manifests in a peculiar way in that, during this time between ages 12 and 13, it energizes the etheric body and intermingles with it.

Again, this is another important point in a child's development. If we handle it correctly, it is expressed in the way a child begins to develop understanding for what acts as impulses in the outside world that are similar to the soul-spiritual impulses that act in the outside world as forces of history, for instance. I have illustrated the mastery of such forces of history in such a way that you can make use of them in primary and middle school curricula. Although you must translate what I have outlined for you into terms understandable to children, if you approach them with the subject of history before they have completed their twelfth year, you will see that no matter how well you managed to make the material understandable, you will still not awaken a correct understanding for historical impulses. Before that age you can teach history in the form of stories such as biographies. Children will understand that. However, before the completion of their twelfth year, children will not understand history and historical connections. Therefore, you would be doing harm if you ignored the necessity of paying heed to this particular time period. At this point in time, a person begins to develop a longing for that which was absorbed as history earlier to be taught formally as a proper subject. For example, if you told a story about some crusader or other earlier, you must now try to refashion it in such a way that children perceive the historical impulse and historical connection associated with the story.

If you have handled things correctly, and then clearly observe that the children are meeting you with understanding from the time they reach age 12, you will say to yourself: Until age 9, I will limit myself mainly to the artistic approach as has been indicated. And, through this approach I will bring in reading and writing and then arithmetic. But I will not begin with natural history until the point in time that was highlighted in the lecture yesterday. As far as history goes, unless it is simply storytelling, I will not begin until after age 12. After age 12 children start to inwardly take part in history and the great historical connections. This will be especially important for the future.

More and more it will become an obvious necessity to educate people in a way that they have a grasp of historical connections, whereas before, people were not educated to have a real understanding of history. People were more like cogs in the wheel of economic and political life. They were like mechanized parts of the socio-economic system, and the demands and interests of this system were met with only the scantest of knowledge about history, etc. It was enough if people knew how to count and about rulers and wars (which is not actually history), a few famous personalities and when they lived, and when the major wars were waged. In the future a special part of the curriculum will have to include the subject of humanity's cultural development. But the curriculum must also include historical impulses and one will have to insert them into the lesson plan at the appropriate time.

After a person has crossed the Rubicon at around age 12, something else is at work that helps further a person's ability to comprehend. Before this age, you can talk about the structure of the human eye in the clearest possible terms, but children will not be able to understand what you have said in the right way until they have reached this particular point in time. What does it really mean when you teach about the structure of the human eye? It means to bring children's attention to how beams of light approach the eye and enter into it, how these light rays are accepted through the eye lens and broken apart, or refracted, and how they pass through the vitreous body of the eye and form as images on the back wall of the eye, and so on. You must describe all this as physical processes. You describe a physical process that takes place within the human being, that is, within a human sense organ. If you wish to describe this process, you must have already developed the concepts that would make it possible for children to receive such a description of the human eye. That means you must have already taught about light refraction. That is very easily explained by showing a lens, explaining about the focus, and showing how the light rays are refracted.

However, one is describing mere physical facts, things that occur outside the human being. This can be done when children are between ages 9 and 12. But using these descriptions of purely physical processes as they apply to organs within a human being should not occur before a child has completed the twelfth year. That is when a child first begins to be able to correctly assess how the outside world works within the human being and how the activity of the outside world is carried into and continued within human beings. Before age 12, children can understand physical processes, but they cannot yet understand the completion of physical processes within the human being.

There is something of a correlation between the ability to understand historical impulses in humanity as a whole and the ability to understand external, physical impulses of nature within the human organism. That which true humanity is lives within historical impulses, but that which is concentrated within these impulses lives as the external course of history and, in turn, affects human beings. When you describe a human eye, the same thing that is active in external nature is also active in the human being. Both processes must be met with the same type of comprehension skills, but this capacity to understand does not begin to develop until age 12.

For this reason it will be necessary to create the lesson plan in such a way that, between ages 9 and 12, children are taught the physical concepts that will allow them to understand the physical human being; that is, besides natural history one also teaches simple physics. However, one should wait to apply the laws of physics to the human being until after age 12, just as one continues to teach history through narrative until age 12 so that one can turn the "story" into "history."

What I have just explained is in reference to the beginning of these matters. Naturally, one continues with the subject of physics after age 12. One should not begin with either physics or natural history before age 9, and history and subjects of a physiological nature, that is, describing human activities, should not be taught before the completion of the twelfth year.

If you adopt the notion that understanding is not merely something that arises in the human intellect, but always includes feeling and will aspects, you will not be very far off. If teachers do not pay attention to such things, it is because they have given themselves over to illusions. One can, in a makeshift way, teach the intellect about history or other subjects of a physiological nature before age 12, but by doing so one spoils a person's human nature. Essentially, a person's innate human nature could be made unfit for the rest of his or her life.

So, for example, between ages 9 and 12 you will find you can gradually begin discussing light refraction and formation of images through a lens or other instruments. During these years between 9 and 12, you will be able to discuss how binoculars work, for instance, and also the workings of a clock, the differences between a pendulum clock and a watch, and other things of this nature. However, before children are 12 years old, you should not apply the concepts of light refraction and image formation to the human eye.

## GA 294, September 1, 1919, Page 136

I have given you these indications because they will allow you to insert some things into the curriculum at the various stages of education that have been highlighted. How many differentiated stages may we expect to encounter during the course of primary and middle school? From what we have learned so far, we see there is an important period of time highlighted around age 9. If we have children in class up to age 9, that previous time period encompasses the first stage of primary/middle school education. How should we teach during this first stage? We take the artistic approach as our starting point. We do painting and drawing as well as music with the class, just as we have discussed. We allow writing skills to gradually develop out of painting-drawing activity. That is to say, we allow written forms to come about gradually out of drawn forms and then we transition into reading.

It is important that you understand the reasons for using this method and not begin with reading and tack writing onto it, but rather transition from writing into reading. In a manner of speaking, writing is something that is more "alive" than reading. Reading is very isolating and pulls someone away from the world, but if we use form drawing to initiate the process of learning to write, we are still imitating world-forms.

Beginning in the second highlighted stage, from ages 9 to 12, we can start to cultivate more self-awareness in children through grammar. By this time, because of the changes they have gone through that I have already characterized for you, children are in a position to receive into their consciousness of self that which grammar has to offer. That is, we now begin with the study of words and also with natural history of the animal kingdom, as I showed you, using a squid, a mouse, and a human being. The plant kingdom follows later. Naturally, instruction in foreign languages continues and feeds into the grammar lessons.

Also at this age we can transition into geometry, while before we kept that aspect which would later become geometry completely in the element of drawing. With drawing we can show a triangle, square, circle, and line. We use drawing to develop the actual geometric forms by drawing them and then saying: "This is a triangle, a square," and so on. But the actual subject of geometry wherein we find the relationships between the various geometric forms does not begin until around age 9.

Last of all we introduce physics and come to the third highlighted stage which lasts until the end of middle school or until age 14 or 15. We also begin here with the study of syntax. Children are only really ready for this at around age 12. Before this age, we instinctively approach children with only those elements of language that allows them to build sentences.

### GA 294, September 2, 1919, Page 150f.

I said before that the subject of geography is first taught beginning in the second stage of primary/middle school, between ages 9 and 12. We can very well begin with geography lessons once children have reached age 9. We must do it only in the right way. Generally, we must see to it that in the future the geography curriculum in primary and middle school (high school as well) encompasses much more than it does at present; geography is all too often put on the back burner, quite neglected. Actually, it ought to be that, in many ways, the acquired learning from all the other subjects converges in geography and all flows together as one. Although I also told you that mineralogy should begin only in the third stage, around age 12, it can still be worked into the geography lessons at an earlier age if it is approached through description and direct observation. Between ages 9 and 12 children can gain an extraordinary amount from geography but only if we go about teaching it in the right way. With geography it is simply a matter of starting with what children already know about the surface of the Earth and what happens there.

### GA 297a, July 28, 1921, Page 81f.

Question and answer period at evening seminar on education
Subject: Religious instruction

*Question:* Speaking of content, how is this instruction oriented to children of anthroposophists?

*Rudolf Steiner:* First and foremost, the material is chosen for its suitability to the children's age. Psychologically speaking, that is always the underlying factor. As with everything else, the material is most effective when it is presented at the exact appropriate age when a child's inner nature resonates with what is being presented. It has to do with the fact that at age 7 or 8 one accomplishes the least with objectively teaching the Catechism or the Gospels or other Bible study. That is simply a law of anthropology. On the other hand, at this age everything religious will be very well received when all material related to ethics and true religion is created with the knowledge of natural processes as its basis. Above all, one can lead children to a sense of the religious by way of imagery from nature.

One can lead children to a real understanding of Christianity beginning only after age 8, or even closer to age 9. That is when they begin to understand what stands behind the figure of Christ, for instance. Children must gradually grow into these concepts that you teach at this time if they are to rightly understand the content of the Gospels. It is good if there is a foundation, but only around age 9 should one appropriately introduce the Gospels and then gradually go further into the deeper mysteries of Christianity. It must be emphasized that even this so-called free religious instruction is thoroughly Christian in the highest sense. The various denominations that take part are introduced to the concept of true Christianity. It is actually true that, when one is a teacher at a Waldorf school, one comes to a belief in Christianity, albeit from an anthroposophical point of view. One has come to Christianity by way of anthroposophy. One will use other words perhaps, but the children will be introduced to true Christianity.

## GA 300b, January 23, 1923, Page 229f.

When we get to the 3rd class we must accommodate the children's condition of mind and soul at that time by having things on the walls that are referred to as "still-life." Naturally, I am not referring to the common still life artworks but rather a realistic representation of living things, but not yet a representation of what is felt. It is good if one brings children only so far as their minds are able to follow along, and for this reason we must leave the things that appeal to the feeling-nature, the animals, until the 4th class. At that time a child's mind and soul begin to relate whatever is represented to the feeling-nature. Children begin to be aware of their feelings even though they are still blunted. Representations of animals such as are found in children's books earlier affected them in such a way that they did not differentiate between realistically portrayed pictures of a cow from one that was carved out of wood, for example. Before the age of between 9 and 10 years old children have no ability to really inwardly differentiate between these two things, but after this age they can do so.

### GA 300c, June 2, 1924, Page 152

Then comes that which follows, the 4th class. It would be good at this time to no longer put off beginning with grammar, not by memorizing rules, but rather by clearly demonstrating how grammar is put to use in the treasure trove of texts the children have already learned. That is how you should begin, inductively, inferring general rules from specific examples. After the rules have been extracted and formed from the texts, one must insist that the children maintain those rules of grammar. That is to say, one may not fall into the extreme of never requiring them to learn rules of grammar, but once the rules have been inductively taught, they should be memorized. Memorizing rules of grammar goes along with the development of the "I"-consciousness between ages 9 and 10. Development of the "I" is encouraged when children are taught rules of grammar logically through the construction of written language.

### GA 300c, June 19, 1924, Page 170f.

Someone asked if there were similar steps to be taken in teaching grammar in foreign languages.

*Dr. Steiner:* You see it is like this: What I have indicated to you is designed for a specific age group. Offering children this special nuance of the soul's constitution simply belongs to this age group. Children most easily learn to let these nuances become active within them through their native language. After they have learned these things in their native language, it would do a lot of good at this age to then tie into that in other languages, something like showing the discrepancies between the native language and other languages when certain moods or sentiments are expressed. One can certainly make very good use of comparisons.

So, one does not begin with teaching grammar until ages 9 to 10. One develops language instruction that is built upon that which has been taught at earlier grade levels purely out of speaking and the feelings associated with speech so that children learn to speak from their feeling-nature. At this stage—which is not completely apparent and not a single point in time but rather quite variable—at this stage between ages 9 and 10, one begins with grammar. The treatment of language in regard to grammar is related to a child's "I" development. But it is not as if one should ask how one develops the "I" through grammar because grammar itself does that. It is not necessary to give any kind of special lessons. One does not begin with grammar earlier, but rather, between ages 9 and 10, one tries to develop grammar solely from out of the substance of language.

## Indications for the Curriculum: Stockmeyer

The 4th class will, again, be a continuation of the 3rd class when it comes to stories and narrative. It would be good if one sees to it that poetry, short poems, in the 1st and 2nd classes, are handled in such a way that children instinctively feel the rhythm, rhyme, and timing of the poem, and in the 3rd and 4th classes one should bring out the inner structure, the inner beauty, of the poem so they can get a feeling for it.

One uses what the children have learned from written stories and descriptions to transition into letter writing of all kinds. At this time one tries to give a clear understanding of the verb tenses and of everything that can be expressed through the different verb forms. That is to say, approximately between ages 9 and 10, children should be given an understanding of the verb tenses so they do not say "the man walked" when they should say "the man had walked." In other words, they should not mix up the past simple and the past perfect tenses, for example.

### GA 301, May 3, 1920, Page 121f.

An attempt has been made to give you indications for the creation of the curriculum and educational goals from various aspects based upon human development. I have specifically characterized the time between ages 6–7 (change of teeth) to ages 14–15 (sexual maturity) as a continuous, defined stage of development that is highlighted by three important transition periods around ages 9, 12, and 14–15 (end of middle school). These three highlighted periods should be decisive factors when structuring the whole curriculum and establishing educational goals for the primary and middle school years.

If one considers knowledge of human development as the standard of control for the curriculum, one will immediately see that, when it comes to the education of human beings, what truly matters is that we bring out all the forces that are present in every human being. If we look at something like this in the right way, we will say to ourselves: "Actually, we must use all of our learning resources and our entire educational life to truly reveal these forces that lie hidden in every human being." It is really not a question of using the forces present in children to get them to learn this or that bit of knowledge. That which we bring as a treasure of knowledge, so to speak, should be used in such a way that only through the effects of this knowledge can the forces present in the inner nature of a child be brought out.

We will not accomplish this if we do not take into consideration how very different the nature of a child is at different stages, up to age 9, between 9 and 12, etc. Above all, we must be aware that real power of differentiation and judgment, what gives a person the ability to judge independently, does not fully appear until after sexual maturity. This capacity begins to appear around age 12 and slowly develops from there. We can say that up to age 9 the inclination of human nature to develop under the direction of authority takes hold in children, but the drive to imitate is still active into the ninth year. After that the desire to imitate disappears, but the inclination for authority remains. However, around age 12, while still influenced by authority which continues into the twelfth year, now the overriding inclination is to make independent judgments.

If we encourage children to exercise their faculty of independent judgment too much before age 12 we do in fact ruin those mental-soul and physical-body forces present in the child. Above all, we kill the human ability to witness, share, and empathize with others using the power of judgment.

## Page 124ff.

At age 9 children experience a real, complete transformation of their being that points to a significant transformation of the life of soul and a significant transformation of the physical, bodily experience. From that time on a person begins to feel separate from the environment. Children learn to differentiate from the world. If we understand how to observe correctly, we would have to say: Until this time of transformation, the world and the "I" more or less flow together in human consciousness. Starting around age 9, approximately, a person differentiates his own self from the world. This must be thoroughly taken into consideration when deciding upon learning materials, subject matter, etc., when teaching children older than 9 years.

Up to this time, we would do well to not mislead children with descriptions and characteristics of things that are detached from the human being or looked at separately from the human being. When we tell a fable or fairy tale, we speak about animals, or perhaps plants, in the same way we would speak about people. In other words, we personify plants and animals. They are rightly personified because children do not yet differentiate their self from the world. For this reason they should see things in the outside world as similar to things they experience within themselves. Please understand that what I am explaining here does not lead to impoverishment in the inner life of a child, but rather enrichment.

My last statement may seem quite paradoxical. Speaking that sentence alone, as I have just done, is in fact paradoxical. But that which is often said about the life of a child is almost always said in the sense of the non-physical aspect of life gradually becoming poorer instead of richer. Just think about what one often hears today, for example, if a child runs into the corner of a table and hits the table in anger because it hurt. One hears it said that children have something in their soul referred to as animism; they see a table, or another inanimate object, as something that is alive and, in a manner of speaking, a child's soul will slip into an object such as a table.

This is, however, an impossible theory. Why? Because children do not see themselves as a living thing and then wish to transfer this living quality into a table so that it becomes personified. No, children do not think of themselves as being any more alive than a table or any other object. When children look at a table, for example, they do not experience any more internally than they do externally by the simple act of looking at it. It is not that children personify objects such as a table, but rather, if I may express it this way, children's personal sense of identity becomes table-like. They do not make out their own personality to be any richer than that of a table. Therefore, when you tell children stories, fairytales, and fables you should tell them only as much as they can grasp from the external world. This is how it must be until they are 9 years old. From age 9 you can begin to count on children learning to differentiate their own self from the external world. That means, from then on we can begin to talk about plants and animals from a natural history perspective.

I have made a great effort to study the effect on children of teaching natural history too early. Studying natural history too early does in fact cause people to be "dry" later on, even to the extent that a careful observer will notice an inclination to yellowing of the skin in people who were taught natural history too early as children.

Around age 9 is the point in time when we may begin to teach natural history. However, we should begin with living things and avoid any formal teaching about the dead, mineral element during this time period. There are two areas of study that include living things that are outside the human sphere: plants and animals.

If one is successful in presenting children with living characteristics of the Earth, plants, animals, and human beings and, in a very simple way, enlivening things that would otherwise be perceived as dead material, something will grow in a person that will bring him or her into a right relationship to the historical life of humanity on the Earth. This should take place in the time period between ages 9 and 12.

At this time children are especially disposed to gradually differentiate their own self from the world but, at the same time, there is a need to absorb into the subconscious the connection between human beings and animals on the one side and that which detaches from human beings on the other side, which is the Earth and the life of the Earth. This is the time when children's feelings and perceptions begin to develop that allows them to grasp history in the right way. Naturally, before age 10 or 11, history should be taught in the form of stories that are biographical in nature. Around age 10 or 11 one adds the subject of history by using the perceptions and feelings that have been absorbed through natural history lessons to, in a manner of speaking, intensively connect with the concepts, ideas, and perceptions that can now enliven history lessons. Starting around age 12, children gradually gain the ability to make real decisions and judgments.

### GA 302, June 19, 1922, Page 133ff.

There are books about experimental education wherein you are urged to take a completely different position. For example, you can find things in books about children's memory and perceptual capabilities that should really be avoided. Experimental education turns things that should really be abolished into the content of the experiment. All the things that should be prevented are included in the experiment. This is something that is so destructive in our present civilization. People want to get to the bottom of how things work with corpses but not how things work with life. They want to know everything about a corpse instead of making the effort to observe how things proceed in life and how actually, in a very subtle, delicate way, children have a kind of awe for everything that happens in the world because they begin to see themselves in it.

At this stage of life a person begins to come into "I"-consciousness. If people see their own selves reflected everywhere and begin to feel and perceive the world of plants and animals, they know something from out of their own being. This inner knowing begins to awaken in children between ages 9 and 10. It will not awaken if one avoids bringing them into artistic activities as well as movement that has a practical purpose. That's what is happening: Today children are not raised to carry out practical activities. Like poor little lambs, they are led into the gymnasium and given orders on how to move their arms and use the various exercise apparati. There is not anything particularly spiritual about these activities even though very many pretty things are said about them. But these activities are not permeated with spirit.

What is the result of this? The result is that at the age when children can most easily be imbued with an inner sense of beauty, that does not take place. Children would so much like to be in awe of things, but the power of wonderment has been destroyed. Take an ordinary lesson plan that is widely used today and you will see the tendencies contained in it are such that when children enter school at age 6 or 7, they are treated in such a way that they become dulled to the experience they should have when they are between ages 9 and 10. Children absolutely do not experience what they should, and because of that, this particular element of experience goes into physicality and sits there in the physical body instead of going into the consciousness. Because this thing that wants to be in the consciousness is now in the physical body, the result is that things begin to change and transform into feelings and appetites in the lower nature so that a person has feelings and forces within about which nothing is known.

So, people go about their lives, but they do not find anything more to life. This is a characteristic of our times. People do not find anything in life because as children they never learned to perceive life as something beautiful. They want only to find everything that will, in the driest sense, enrich the intellect. But they never discover the hidden, secret beauty that is everywhere, and so their connection to life dies away. This is the way of our culture. The connection human beings have to nature is cut off. If one is aware of this, one knows that what matters is finding the right words for a child around age 9. Children of this age are expecting something. They want to be amazed about something. If one does not meet this expectation, then actually a lot will have been destroyed. One must learn to observe children and be able to feel one's way into their internal being. One must not do external experiments, but really get inside a child's nature.

It really is true that one must say: Human beings develop in such a way that they set out on a specific course in life from the moment something emerges out of the bottom layers of speech, in a manner of speaking, that tells children they are "I." Learning to say "I" happens relatively early but it is still something dreamlike and continues to live in children in that state. Children are then brought to us in the school, and since they have now entered school, we must turn them around because they want to go in a different direction. We must guide them into artistic activities. After we have worked with children in this way for a time, they will find their way back and again come to the point in their life where they have learned to say "I." Things continue for a time until later, through sexual maturity, they again come to this point. We can prepare children for this moment if, between ages 9 and 10, we lead them into a sense of amazement and wonder for the world. If we cultivate a sense of beauty so that it becomes more conscious, then we have prepared them to learn to love the world in the right way when they enter puberty. In this way children develop the right sense of love for the world.

It is not only a matter of love for another person; that is only one aspect. Love is that which extends over everything and is the deepest impulse to act. We should do what we love. Duty and obligation should merge with love. We should like what we have to do. This will develop as it should only if we guide children in the right way. Throughout primary and middle school, we must see to it that we help children develop a feeling for beauty in the right way. In a certain way they already have a sense for truth when they come to us, but a sense for beauty must be taught in the way I have indicated.

## GA 303, January 1, 1922, Page 177ff.

When a child has completed the ninth year, there comes an important period of development during the time between ages 9 and 10. This developmental moment can be identified if one notices that the change of teeth and a child's desire for authority that is associated with that event essentially remains unchanged until he or she has completed the ninth year. Children do not wish to exert their individuality against authority. They accept that which is given from authority as a matter of course and have a need to adhere to authority. But with the completion of the ninth year, something very special occurs. From this point in time onward, in a certain way, children want authority to be justified.

Please do not misunderstand me. A child does not intellectually weigh the question of whether authority is justified or not. However, within his or her whole life of feeling lies something that works in such a way that authority must be preserved by its own qualities, how authority figures are positioned in life and how secure they are within themselves. From this time onward, children have an especially sensitive feeling for this and this is expressed through the fact that, even objectively, they experience a turning point in their lives at this time that absolutely must be taken into consideration if their education is to proceed in a healthy way. Up to this time children differentiate from the environment very little. As far as children's perceptions are concerned, they and the world belong together.

When one characterizes these things, it is necessary to express them somewhat radically, but I ask you to please take these radical characterizations in the way they are intended. For example, one must say that before the end of a child's ninth year, there is no such thing as humans, animals, plants, and minerals, but only beings in general. Of course, when one says it like this, it must not be taken to mean that a child is unable to tell the difference between people and lilies. However, in a certain way, what I have said stands, but also, in a certain way, education must surely not dogmatically receive these things that have been expressed in quite a radical way. Life sees to it that everything balances out and nothing appears with the sharp contours that a pedantic stickler might wish to see.

With the completion of a child's ninth year, for instance, something comes to an end in a very pronounced way that is always presented in a false light by the science of child development. For example, one may observe that if a child runs into the corner of a table, he or she will turn around and hit the table. Scientists explain that the child is personifying the table, turning it into a living thing that should be punished. When things like this are said, it shows the shallow assumptions that have been made about a child's state of mind. It is absolutely not the case that a child personifies the table. What is happening is that the child has not yet learned to differentiate between living and non-living things. The process of personification is totally absent in the life of a child. Children interact with the outside world in quite a generalized way and see themselves in this world in such a way that they really do not differentiate much between their own self and the surroundings. Therefore, the time after the completed ninth year is especially important because that is a very critical transition point in which questions stream out of a child, mountains of questions that all have to do with perceptually differentiating the self from the surroundings, and also from teachers.

Until this time children have little sense of whether a teacher is a clumsy person, for instance, who runs into things and drops the chalk, etc. Children have very little capability of observing things such as the preacher who developed a habit of touching his nose after every sentence, which greatly amused his congregation. Before the completion of the ninth year, children do notice such things, but they do not leave a deep impression. It is a mistake to believe that children simply do not notice. However, after the completion of the ninth year they begin to very sharply observe such things. At age 10 or 11 they observe less closely than the year before. Now, children notice things, and they wrap up their observations into a whole barrage of questions that are burdening their soul at this point in time. These questions may not be expressed verbally but they are there. Children ask (not intellectually, but with the feeling-nature) if their teachers are smart and skillful, if they feel secure in their standing in life (very important), and know what they want. Above all, children have a very fine sense of the state of a teacher's soul.

A skeptic has a completely different effect on children than a person who believes (in the right sense of the word). There is something that comes through the voice of a skeptic that sounds very different from that of a person of belief. Children worry about such things between ages 9 and 10. There is much here that lies in the life of a person that is very individual and which must be taken into consideration. An evangelical-orthodox teacher has a very different effect on a child at this point in time than someone of a Catholic persuasion simply because of their varying attitudes of soul.

There is something else that comes into play here. This transitional moment in a child's life is expressed in the most varied ways depending on race and/or nationality. It can even be said that some nationalities reach this point a little later and some earlier. One cannot generalize much except to say that teachers must approach this time period with their full ability for tactful understanding so they can really see this turning point in a child's development. An enormous amount depends on teachers turning their most acute, apt attention to their pupils at this time. In Waldorf schools there is great importance attached to this. There are discussions about every single child in the weekly teacher's conferences. As the schools grow it will become necessary to come up with other means, but always we must try to learn as much as possible about the special individuality of each child. One can learn quite a lot, especially if one takes it upon oneself to study the imponderables of growing human beings.

**Page 180ff.**

From everything I have described, you can be certain that during this time it is inevitable that children will approach a teacher and ask all manner of questions. It does not really matter what the questions are or even what answers are given. The only thing that really matters is that, through this almost indefinable quality of relationship that must develop between children and teachers at this time, children's minds are instilled with an outlook that resonates with their feeling-nature: "Up to now I have looked up to my teacher. I cannot do that anymore without knowing that my teacher looks up to something that is in some way justified." Especially curious children may even follow a teacher outside of school and notice everything he or she does. To take all of this into consideration is incredibly important. But the one thing upon which all else depends is that one recognizes this moment and realizes that children will now approach their teacher and that what plays out between them requires trust, increasingly more conscious trust. How teachers act during this time will influence a great deal for the rest of children's later lives. Whether they become a rudderless adult or someone who stands secure in life often depends upon whether a teacher found the right, positive approach in his or her interactions with them at this moment in their development.

One could certainly ask: How are children actually dependent upon the environment when they are so extraordinarily reliant upon teachers acting in a certain way when they are between ages 9 and 10? We cannot shed light on these things without getting into questions of a person's destiny, karmic questions. And we will get into that during the last part of this presentation. But for the time period we have been discussing, what matters most is that a child finds someone (one person or several, it makes little difference) who will, in a certain way, remain as an image for the rest of a person's life.

There are few people who pay attention to what I am about to say, but again and again, and at specific periods in life, the effects of childhood appear in that person's adult life, and the image that appears at various times, again and again, from this particular turning point in a child's life holds brilliant and marvelous significance for that adult life. In later life when this image appears, in dreams or a waking state, whether one looks at it sympathetically or antipathetically is extremely important. The sympathy or antipathy is not important in and of itself. What matters is that there is something in the mind of a child that will later result in sympathy or antipathy.

I will certainly not claim that the whole process I have described here, recalling the turning point between ages 9 and 10, is explicitly lodged in one's consciousness. Sometimes it lies almost completely in the subconscious, but the process still must take place. It always does. People who are given to lively, active dreams will almost regularly see appear the personality of someone who was there for them during this period between ages 9 and 10, someone who developed a personal relationship with them, helped them, admonished them, awakened a sense of trust and was on their side. Children need this during the time between ages 9 and 10. It is connected with the objective transition taking place within a child. Whereas before this time children did not differentiate their own self from the environment, they now experience the need to have the inner sense that they are human, self-contained individuals standing before the world.

**Page 184ff.**

If you teach children only what you have read in books, you come off sounding like a very dry person no matter how lively and engaged you are outwardly. It is almost as if you do not have living skin but are wrapped in parchment paper because, you see, one always carries something of the remains of what one has learned in a purely traditional, intellectual way. On the other hand, what one has thought of oneself still has room for growth and fresh life in it, and that has an effect on children.

Therefore, the desire to create your own stories about the whole world of plants, animals, and the Sun and stars as they are found in fairytales must be present in teachers if you wish to teach children of this age group. There will be a very positive effect on children if teachers do the strenuous work of preparing a story of their own and enter the classroom eager to share their creation with the class. Of course, the story will not really be finished until one sees the satisfied and joyful faces of the children radiating back at the teacher. Actually, up to the completion of the ninth year, everything children learn about plants, animals, minerals, Sun, Moon, mountains, and rivers should be taught in this form because in this way children unite with the world. World and child, child and world—it is all one at this age.

Something occurs with the big change that has been identified around age 9 to 10. Children want to be individuals in their own right. They learn to differentiate their own self from the world. Teachers now have the possibility, as well as the responsibility to introduce children to nature and the environment. At this time one must focus on something which can be described as the radical difference between introducing children to the world of plants and introducing them to the world of animals. Human beings need to have these two kingdoms of nature introduced in entirely different ways.

Certainly, children can be introduced to both of them between the ages of 9 and 11, but one must use different approaches. It is really a terrible thing to approach children of this age with a plant that is detached from the soil, a being that has been ripped out of the ground. This forces the perception that the plant, torn from the soil, is not an independent being. One must get a sense for the whole plant world in the same way one perceives a human hair to be connected to the whole human organism, for example. A human hair that has been plucked out and is just lying there makes no sense. There is no reality to it. The hair could never have come about through just the forces present within a single hair. In the same way, a plant is something that could never exist on its own if it was ripped from the soil. Plants belong on the face of the Earth. Plants and soil belong together. There is something else that happens which we will soon see, but for now, suffice it to say, plants and soil belong together.

Therefore, wherever possible, it is important to present children with a view that is appropriate for their sensibilities, wherein plants and soil are together. In that way one awakens a feeling for how roots, with their unique characteristics, belong in the ground. Children must not be given an abstract, intellectual view, but rather one that appeals to their feeling-nature, a view of how roots are different if they are in dry soil, moist soil, near to a cliff face, or close to the sea. First of all, children must learn to see plants as being completely connected to the soil. All vegetation must be seen as a piece of that which comes out of the Earth.

One must also call forth a feeling for the contrast between the roots, which belong to the Earth, and the flowers and fruit, which are driven forth by the Sun. One must guide children from the Earth to the Sun by way of the flowering plants. Children must get a feeling for how flowers are able to blossom through the surrounding warmth of the Sun and how flowering and bearing fruit is, in actual fact, a plant's way of gradually emancipating itself from the earth element. Earth, plant growth, and the effect of the Sun on the earth element all belong together and they must be shown that way to children. One could say that children should have such a concept of plant life that if one were to describe a plant to them without its relationship to soil and Sun, they would feel inner sorrow, as if the plant were ripped from the ground.

**Page 224**

Naturally, children learn their mother tongue without any kind of attention to grammar, and this is, of course, the way they should learn it. It is the same when they enter school and are taught foreign languages. They should be taught without the encumbrance of grammar lessons, albeit in a somewhat more mature emulation of the way the mother tongue is learned.

However, when children reach the turning point between ages 9 and 10, life simply demands that they are taught some knowledge of grammar for the sake of correct development, albeit not pedantically. At this age children must find the transition into "I" development. Everything must be learned in a more conscious way than before. Therefore, one must bring the thinking element into the already present feeling element of the languages the children already speak, not pedantically, but through stimulating, practiced discovery of the rules of grammar. Children must be taught some grammar so that when they reach the time between ages 9 and 10 they will not say to themselves: "How do I say this? How do I say this?" without having some kind of logical frame of reference. You must understand that there are two elements in languages that are always intertwined: a thinking element and a feeling element. I would like to illustrate this with a quote from Goethe's *Faust*:

Gray, dear friend, is every theory,
And green the life of a golden tree.

**Page 225**

Now, what is really at the heart of the above phrase? It is this: In this sentence the feeling element of the language on the one side and the thinking element on the other side are both very strongly represented. When he says "a golden tree," he means a tree that one likes as much as gold, whereby the word "golden" is not referring to the look of the tree but the feeling one gets when one looks upon its unique, shining brilliance. That is to say, a golden tree is that which one feels, the same feeling evoked when looking at gold. These words are written completely for the feeling they invoke. But the word "green" denotes an actual tree that can be seen. There, logic has been taken into account. "Theory" is not something one sees, yet many people, whether it is warranted or not, feel what they can feel when there is fog in London, for instance. So, feeling can be carried over to the experience of "theory." And, again, the word "gray" is simply representing the feeling element of the language.

These elements of language, feeling and thinking, are everywhere mixed up together. There is much that has already been stultified in today's language, but in earlier epochs language was an active, creative element and that is how the feeling element was brought into the thinking element of language.

Before age 9 a child's relationship to language is completely in the realm of feelings. But a child's consciousness of self could not develop if we did not bring something of the thinking element into it. Therefore it is so very important to bring the thinking element into language by teaching rules of grammar in the appropriate way, beginning with the native language but then perhaps following with grammar in foreign languages as well.

The following should be taken into consideration: Between ages 9 and 10, children should get the feeling they have penetrated somewhat into understanding language in the way that I have described. In this way one can guide children into a real feeling for the grammar of language. By around age 11 the children should have developed a feeling for the beauty of language, an aesthetic perception of language. Also around age 11, children should make an effort to speak in an acceptable manner; what one could call "proper speech."

### GA 304, November 11, 1921, Page 106

There is something we must understand clearly: What you teach an 8-year-old today may not be sharply contoured and shaped but must contain an inner capacity for growth. It must be able to become something completely different when a person is 40 years old. You must be able to look at children in terms of their entire lifespan. Those who do not give proper credence to the authority principle during the childhood years have most likely never experienced what it actually means at age 35 to remember something from the distant past that causes someone to "get" some idea about history, geography, etc., or perhaps something that has to do with life itself, which was accepted on the authority of a beloved teacher. At the time, the child may not have understood, but it was accepted on the authority of a teacher nevertheless. When ideas and concepts like these arise and one understands them after a period of decades, that is what is referred to as an enlivening principle. It calls forth an undefined feeling that does not even need to be brought to consciousness. You have something from your childhood years that is a living presence, even in your life of soul. In this regard, we must absolutely be able to pursue the forces of growth in nature.

### Page 112ff.

Between ages 9 and 10 something extraordinarily important happens: Children actually begin to differentiate from the environment. During this year we can begin to teach about the nature of plants and animals, which is independent of the human being. At this time something very remarkable happens within the child. The most important thing is that teachers really understand how to observe that in one child this happens a little earlier, in another child a little later, but something is happening in the deepest nature of a child: A child becomes a different being. Through the feeling-nature, not the intellect, children learn to differentiate their own self from the world.

If one observes this time period correctly, through the fact that one finds the right words and behavior during this year, one has done something that is of enormous importance for the rest of a child's life. During this period of time it is possible to bring a kind of desolation to children so that they will go through their lives living in doubt, dissatisfaction, and inner desolation. Or, if one has the inner vitality and enough empathy to understand what is happening at this point in time, one can do something for a child that holds enormous significance for the rest of that life. In a certain way one must really delve into the being of a child and find there the right words and actions when interacting with a child. Correct observation of the exact point in time when a child experiences this change is especially important in the Waldorf method of education.

From this time onward it will be very possible to teach things that include simple descriptions of plants, animals, etc., whereas before these things had to be treated in stories and fables. Between ages 10 and 11, actually beginning more around age 11, one can begin to teach some inorganic physics. Only then, after the children have internally absorbed all the things that will put them on the right path in life, can one introduce subjects of the non-living by way of the living. That is how one leads the children up to the age of sexual maturity and the end of middle school. I have only mentioned a few characteristic things that I have chosen as examples.

In our time, puberty is discussed, philosophized, and psycho-analyzed so much. But the real crux of the matter is that one sees that an important life stage is reached with puberty exactly the same as with the change of teeth. Puberty itself is only a part of the metamorphosis that encompasses all of a person's humanness at this age. What happens with the change of teeth is that a child's inner soul forces are released, the same forces that were working in the physical organism before.

Between ages 8 and 15, approximately, one is dealing with trying to correctly help children develop from within in the way I have discussed with you today. With puberty children enter into the time period in which they can, in a manner of speaking, begin to rightly stand in the external world with their own powers of judgment. While before they brought their own being up to the surface from out of the depths of their organism, now they are able to take in, as such, the spiritual aspect of the world. This is one of the greatest challenges of education and also one of the greatest problems of a truly living educational method—how to educate children between ages 8 and 15, and how to bring them in a very natural way to the age when they actually begin to gain an independent, individual relationship to the world, of which physical love is only one part. What comes to the forefront with physical love, love of another human being, is really only a small part of human social life. We must bring children to the point that they are internally mature enough to follow things of the external world with interest and not skim things they should feel drawn to in love.

We must help children develop into social beings up to the time of sexual maturity. However, in a certain way, we must also help them develop piety and devotion, not devotion in the sense of moral cowardice, but in the sense of earnest development of that within oneself through which a person grows into the knowledge that everything external of a physical nature is permeated with spirit, so that someone will not be content with mere observation of the outer, physical things of the senses, but will be able to see the spiritual foundation of everything.

During this time when children come to meet us with their own being and believe in our authority, we must carry within ourselves that which, for a child, is, in a certain way, the world. If a child finds a world in us, a world in which we are the teacher, he or she is well prepared to stand before the world as a devoted, social being. We discharge the children from our authority, which gave them their world, into the real world itself.

Let me say a few words about some of the most significant problems of awareness and insight. Those who develop powers of independent judgment in children too early bring forces of death instead of life into a developing child. Only those who use authority in such a way that a child's natural belief is really awakened are doing and saying the correct things. To be sure, those who are, in this sense, the representatives of the world to children do not prepare them through mastery of the intellect or any kind of powers of judgment, but rather through their own living human qualities, to further unfold in the world as living human beings. Life must be developed through life. We must not start from an aspect of abstract purity, abstract intellectualized concepts, but rather, we must bring children a world in the form of a living person. That is how we help children become true citizens of the world.

All of this can be characterized in a few lines, but it is assumed that one is able to see into the details and singularities of developing forces within a child, I would say, on a day to day basis. The way in which one carries something through the door of the classroom, so to speak, has an effect on children's being able to grow into their own lives through the life of a teacher. One need not bother with such amateurish ideas as "learning should make children happy." Today, many people use such phrases. Just try it and see how far you get with such an abstract principle! In many ways learning cannot make children happy. However, through the life that one brings to schoolwork, one should bring children to the point that they at least approach things that do not necessarily make them happy with a certain curiosity and appetite for knowledge. The way a teacher approaches this and handles it is an indication to children of just how much they can know through their teacher.

Then comes the natural development of a sense of duty: conscientiousness. We are now manifesting something that lies much deeper than merely within the area of education. With this we are featuring something that could come out of a truly spiritually-based method of education and mature into something that permeates our entire cultural life.

### GA 304, November 24, 1921, Page 165f.

Yesterday I indicated that between ages 9 and 10 is an important point in child development and how very much depends upon how teachers are able to discover the innermost needs of the soul of each individual child and then appropriately handle the situation. However, this time period in child development must also be sharply observed in respect to something else because at this time children actually learn to rightly separate their own self from the environment. They separate through the feeling- and will-natures, and through their power of judgment. Children only learn to truly differentiate from the environment through complete inner independence at the time of sexual maturity.

However, during the development that takes place between ages 9 and 10, approximately, the nuances of this separation become apparent. And, that is why it is so important to keep an eye out for this moment because one must keep the child well in hand up to puberty. Nevertheless, as I explained yesterday, you should allow for some changes to enter into how you handle the situation. Up to this point it is best if children are taught in such a way that no claim is made that would require them to differentiate from the environment in any way. It is always a detriment if we teach natural history before age 10 or 11, or any subject that points children in the direction of objectivity and makes it necessary to differentiate their own self from the environment. The more one can personify the environment, speak imaginatively about it, and teach with an artistic approach, the better it is for a developing child, and the more a child's will-nature will be able to open up and be internalized.

This will-nature of a child can be deepened through everything that is musical. From about age 7 or 8 onward, music provides internalization and nuance of feeling. The will is made strong through all other activities of a pictorial, artistic nature, as long as they are appropriate for a child's age. One must be absolutely clear that speaking about plants, animals, and lifeless things in nature should be done in such a way that children do not feel they are separate from these things. They should feel that, in a certain way, these things are only continuations of their own being. Personification of external things and facts is very appropriate at this age.

## Page 170ff.

Up to age 10 or 11, eurythmy is an especially important resource because it works retroactively on the spirit and soul and becomes an important aid in later years when children learn to differentiate from the environment at approximately age 10 to 11. However, one must pay very close attention to how this differentiation makes its appearance.

At first, one will have to be careful not to introduce too early things in which only the intellect, the ability to understand intellectual concepts, is active. Therefore, the study of animals and plants should always precede the study of minerals, physics, and chemistry. In respect to plants and animals, one will see that children learn to differentiate from the environment in a variety of ways. Within their own being, around age 10 or 11, children feel they are closer to the animal world than to that of plants. Plant life feels like something that is revealed from inside the world. The animal world feels like something with which one can empathize and that, in a certain way, the being of animals is similar to human beings.

This must be thoroughly accounted for in the curriculum and in your teaching. For this reason, that which one teaches children of this age about plants must be taught in such a way that plants are situated with the Earth. In plants one must see something that is like an organism growing out of the Earth. The earth element is always connected with plants, and earthly development throughout vast spans of time is revealed by the plants of those different eras. This must be treated in various ways. That is to say, as far as possible, look at plants in relation to time.

It is easy to get off track if one strives to achieve vivid clarity, which is justified in other areas, in an area such as this. One pays too little attention to the fact that the Earth and its plant growth are a unity. Perhaps it appears paradoxical, but as little as one would examine the hair of an animal by itself instead of being a part of the whole animal organism, so should one treat the Earth as a whole organism and plants as a part of that organism. If one represents the plant world in this way, what children can observe of the plant kingdom is correctly disassociated from them.

In contrast, something completely different should preside over the study of the animal kingdom. In a manner of speaking, children have a bridge of feeling to animals, a soul-bridge that should be taken into consideration. Today, the views held by older natural philosophers in this regard are often dismissed with a smile. This happens also in Goethe's way of looking at the animal kingdom.

However, when one turns one's attention to one animal form or another, we find that with a lion, for instance, the chest region with the heart is especially prominent. With another animal it might be the digestive organs, or another animal might have especially predominantly formed teeth, or horns, etc. The various animal forms are studied as expressions of individual organs. One could say there are head-animals, chest-animals, and limb-animals. One can divide the animal forms further still and then one has the whole. If one takes all the individual animal forms together, one has a synthesis, in a manner of speaking. In this synthesis, all of the individual qualities that are at the forefront withdraw their prominence in order to serve the whole. This is how one comes to the human form. In external form, the human being is, in a manner of speaking, the aggregation of the whole animal kingdom.

One can definitely instill in children this understanding of the aggregation of the whole animal kingdom in the human being. Then something extraordinarily significant has been done, because if one has correctly presented the plant kingdom on the one side and the animal kingdom on the other, children will, in a manner of speaking, see the whole animal kingdom as an outspread, dispersed human being and the plant kingdom as something belonging organically with the whole Earth. If one enlivens tangible demonstrations and explanations of plant and animal studies in this way, one is, at the same time, taking into account how people should position themselves into the world through their inner being. Then they will grow into the world in the right way at the age when they are beginning to learn to differentiate their individual self from the world, when subject and object begin to separate.

This is how one brings it about that the world is separated from the human being through the study of plants in the right way, and, on the other hand, a bridge to the world is formed from out of the human being, which must be there if any kind of right feeling and love for the world is to develop. To bring that about requires teaching children that the animal kingdom is like the human being all spread out into different parts. Organically, in this living way, one imparts to children their relationship with the world. Beginning around age 11, one has actually the first opportunity to transition into purely intellectual aspects of life without negatively affecting a child's development.

If this course that I have spoken about today is followed, we transition from a culture of the will-nature into cultivation of the feeling-nature by developing children's relationship to the plant and animal kingdoms and teaching them natural history. Something is affected in a child that reaches the feeling-nature. Children learn to relate to plants and animals not only theoretically and by imagining things about them, they establish a relationship with the natural environment. This is tremendously important. If we, in this way, through external movement and correct guidance, have brought children through the culture of the will-nature up to about age 11, we will then find the transition to the actual culture of the intellectual nature. Children's intellectual nature can now express itself as we move on to provide more learning resources and teaching materials that have to do with lifeless nature.

### GA 305, August 21, 1922, Page 101

Above all, we must take into account that, at the beginning of the phase between the change of teeth and puberty, children cannot yet differentiate between their inner humanness and the external environment. For children up to age 9 or 10, both grow together as one. Nature just is. Children inwardly feel this or that. Let us say a child looks at an external process such as a sunrise or something like that. The same forces a child supposes to be present when something causes unhappiness or pain are also thought by a child to be present in the Sun and Moon, trees and plants. We should not try to talk a child out of this assumption. We should put ourselves in a child's place and, before the age of 9 or so, we should treat everything in education as if no boundary yet exists between inner human nature and external nature. This we can do only if we teach as imaginatively as possible by treating plants, the Sun and Moon like people and allowing them to talk to each other.

In other words, we assign human qualities to everything. Today, there is real skepticism about so-called anthropomorphism. But children who have not experienced anthropomorphism in their relationship to the environment will be missing a part of what it is to be human in their later life. Teachers must have an inclination to also imagine themselves into this environment in such a lively, soul-spiritual way that children can absolutely go along as best as they can with what is already present within them.

## Page 104

Therefore, we start mainly with fairytale stories and stories of our own invention that relate to nature. At first, we teach neither languages nor any other subject, but rather we simply let the world come alive through imagery. And, in the best way, such instruction from out of pictorial imagery falls into line with that which leads to writing and reading.

Between ages 9 and 10, approximately, we bring children to the point of being able to express themselves through writing, and also to read, as much as is beneficial for children of this age. With that we reach the point in a child's life that I have already indicated which is approximately between ages 9 and 10.

This important time in a child's life also has an outward manifestation. There appears a noticeable difference between boys and girls. I will speak further about this and what it means for schools that have coed classes, as is the case in a Waldorf school. One must be aware that an important differentiation between boys and girls happens at this time. Around age 10, or thereabouts, girls begin to grow physically at a faster rate than boys. The boys' growth rate stays behind and the girls overtake them. When the boys and girls reach puberty, the boys' growth rate overtakes the girls. That is to say, at this age boys grow faster.

Between their ninth and tenth years, just from the outward physical differences between boys and girls it is already apparent that one is entering a significant period in a child's life. What comes to expression from within a child is that, actually, he or she is learning to differentiate from the rest of nature. Before this time period, children really have no concept of a plant, but rather of something that is green with red flowers and has a little spirit inside, just like they perceive themselves to have a little spirit inside. Children begin to get a sense of a plant, this living being, when they are around 9 or 10 years old. Through empathy, one must be able to discern when this is happening. So, starting only at this age may one create the lessons in such a way that one speaks about the natural environment as an external world.

Then one can begin with what is thought of as a regular school subject: the study of plants—botany, for instance. In the case of botany, I can demonstrate to you how one realistically, and in the best sense of the word, should conduct a well-thought-out course of lessons. If we start by showing a single plant by itself, we are doing something completely unnatural, for an individual plant does not represent a whole. A plant, especially if it is uprooted, is not anything whole. In our time of stark realism and materialism, people actually have very little true sense for the material and naturalistic; otherwise they would feel what I have just explained. Is a plant something whole? No, if we pull it out of the soil and lay it out here, it will very quickly wither and die. It is not in the nature of plants to be torn from the soil. A plant is able to live only in the soil, together with it. A rock is something whole in and of itself. A rock can be put down anywhere and it remains the same. A plant cannot be put down just anywhere, for it would not be the same anymore. A plant is what it is only in conjunction with the soil and only when it is together with the forces that spring forth from the Earth and all the energies from the Sun that happen to fall on that part of the Earth. That is when a plant can be seen as something whole. Looking at a plant isolated from the soil is as absurd as pulling out a single hair and looking at it as if it were a thing in and of itself. The hair can exist and be understood only in connection with an organism. In other words, when studying plants one cannot start from an individual plant, that is to say, from the being of a plant. One must begin with the landscape and geography that is present at a certain place on the Earth. Everything to do with plants must be handled in connection with the whole Earth.

When we talk about the Earth, we speak as physicists, or, at the very most, geologists. We imagine that the Earth is an enclosed totality of physical and mineral forces and that it could exist even if no plants, animals, or people were living upon it. This, however, is an abstraction. The Earth that physicists and geologists have in mind is an abstraction. In reality it does not exist. The only Earth that exists is the one covered in plants everywhere. We must be aware that when we describe something geologically, we are actually describing an apparitional abstraction merely for the sake of the convenience of our intellect.

However, from the beginning, we should not teach children this bodiless abstraction. For children, the Earth should be made into a living organism, beginning with the landscape with which they are familiar. Just as one would show children an animal upon which hair grows, and not try to make them understand a hair when they know nothing of the animal, so one must first present the Earth as a living organism and then show how the plants live and grow upon it. That is how one teaches about plants; first children are taught about the Earth as a living organism, beginning with the piece of it with which they are most familiar. Of course, this is also an abstraction since one particular landscape cannot exist alone, without other landscapes on the Earth. However, one must just be aware that we are starting with something incomplete and lacking. In spite of this and, again, from out of the whole of the imagination, we can gradually awaken in children what is necessary to teach them about plants.

Through this we gradually bring children closer to the external world. They develop a sense for the term "objectivity" and begin to live into the earthly reality. The best way to accomplish this is by introducing the world of plants in this natural way.

Children must be introduced to the animal world in a completely different way, as well as a little later. Once again, to describe individual animals is something that is completely inorganic. Actually, one could almost say that it is pure chance that a lion is a lion and a camel is a camel. Yes, in the observation of a lion, or even a pride of lions, no matter how well and imaginatively described, it will seem very arbitrary to children. The same goes for camels. For one thing, such an observation makes no sense if one is starting from the standpoint of a living domain of nature. So, what is it with the animals?

Now, those who approach the subject of animals not with abstract intellectualism, but rather with imaginative vision, will find a piece of humankind in every animal. One animal will have very strongly developed legs, whereas in the human being the legs do not dominate but rather serve the whole organism. Another animal will have the sense organs, or just one sense organ, developed to the extreme. One animal will snuffle and root around in the ground while another has especially sharp eyes when it is flying in the air. And if the whole animal world is put together, then we find that an aggregation, a synthesis, of exaggerated parts of the animals gives us a picture of the human being. If I put together a synthesis of all the animals, I end up with the whole human being.

Whatever characteristics or group of faculties are present in the human being, they are one-sidedly, outwardly developed in one or another species of animal. When we study a lion, for instance, we do not need to explain this to children. We can explain using simple imagery. With a lion, we find that especially the chest organs of the human being, the heart organs, are one-sidedly developed in a lion. The organs of digestion in the human being are one-sidedly developed in a cow. If I look at the white corpuscles swimming around in our blood, for example, I see indications of the simplest, most primitive animals. The whole of the animal kingdom together constitutes the human being, a synthesis, not added together like a summary, but rather woven together as a composite.

### GA 307, August 13, 1923, Page 157f.

When one transitions to reading, basically, there is nothing to do except see to it that the children recognize with their head forces, their thinking, what they have already learned by their whole body's working through activity (writing), so that reading becomes a remembrance of an activity that has been performed by oneself. This is enormously important. It spoils human development if children are led directly to something abstract (reading) and learn to carry out any kind of activity through a taught concept. In contrast, when the activity is stimulated first and then the concept developed from out of the activity—this always leads to healthy development. Reading is something that lives completely in the mental realm of concepts and therefore should be developed after writing, not before. Otherwise, one will bring children much too early into a kind of head development (intellect) instead of into a development of the whole human being.

So, you see how, basically, through this method, all instruction can be guided into the sphere of the whole human being, into the sphere of the artistic. This must be the aim of all the other lessons as well, up to the age of about 9½. Everything must be oriented to pictorial imagery and rhythm and measure. Anything else is premature.

Before this age, it is completely impossible to teach the child anything that conveys a clear distinction between a person and the external world. Children begin to differentiate from the outside world between the ages of 9 and 10, approximately. When a child first enters school, teaching is a matter of transforming all outside things into living beings of a sort. One does not simply talk about plants, but rather one speaks of plants as living beings that say things to you and to each other, so that, basically, all the lessons having to do with nature and human beings are drenched in fantasy. The plants talk, the trees talk, the clouds talk. And, actually, at this age, children should not feel there is any difference between themselves and the world. We must instill in children the sense that just as they can speak, so everything in the surroundings can speak also.

The more we achieve this merging of children with their whole environment, the more we are able to talk about everything—plants, animals, and rocks—as if everywhere there is something that is meaningfully speaking, spiritual, and interwoven that is wafting around them, and the more we are able to meet that which their innermost being demands from us at this age.

These are the years when the sentient life of the soul must flow into the processes of breathing, blood circulation, and formation of blood vessels—indeed into the whole human organism. This way of educating that is appropriate to children's nature will, in actuality, correctly address the life of feeling for our time so that children, in a natural way, strongly, organically, develop the life of feeling.

It is of tremendous benefit to children if we develop the feeling element along with writing and then allow just a hint of the intellect to shine through in the remembrance of the writing activity that is recognized in the activity of reading. Here is a quiet hint of the intellect. This is the best way for us to lead children into their ninth year.

Above all, between ages 7 and 9 or 9½, all instruction should appeal to the feeling life so that all the forms of the alphabet letters really enter into the life of feeling. With this action one does something tremendously significant because if we teach writing based on mere mechanics, teaching a certain set of lines for each letter, there is a hardening effect; in a certain way we make children too strongly aligned with the forces of bones, cartilages, and tendons in relation to the rest of their organism. This method appeals to body mechanics instead of including the eyes in the process.

If we appeal to the eyes as well, which are of course connected with the moving hand, through artistic development, the alphabet letters will not be simply mechanically reproduced by directing hand movements, but rather, they will be produced in such a way that the eyes will take pleasure in looking at the result of their own activity. In this way the soul-nature is engaged appropriately and the feeling life can develop in the right way at this age when it can best stream into the physical organism with health-giving properties.

**Page 171ff.**

Beginning with the physical organization, we teach children about the threefold nature of the human being in a simple way. Then, going through the animals, we show how they each one-sidedly develop some aspect of their physical being that is harmoniously integrated into the whole physical nature of the human being. In this way one can discover how certain animals one-sidedly develop the chest organs and other animals the digestive organs, etc. In some animals, birds, for example, the transformation of certain organs is present, such as a bird's craw, which is a metamorphosis of digestive organs. In this way one can represent each animal species as the one-sided development of an organ system in the human being. The human being can be represented as a synthesis of the whole animal kingdom. The whole of the animal world, with its diversity of forms, can be represented as the human being spread out like a fan over the Earth.

If one is successful in conveying this picture, children will understand the animals as similar to humans that have one-sidedly developed organ systems; one organ system exists as this animal species and another organ system exists as another animal species. When the children are nearing age 12, one can come back around to the subject of the human being. They will naturally understand how the human being, since he bears his spirit within himself, is an artistic synthesis, an artistically unified expression of all the individual human-type fragments which the various animal species of the world represent individually.

Human beings are such an artistic synthesis because they carry their spirit within them. Through their spirit, human beings harmonize into an interrelated, whole system; by a complex process, the lower animals' organization is transformed into the human head organization, which is appropriately integrated into the chest organization, which is appropriately formed to suit the other organs. The human being also has within that which belongs to the fish species as well as the higher animals, but it is all organized into a harmonious, complete physical being. Through their spirit, human beings have emerged as a complete synthesis of a physical being put together from the individual fragments represented by each animal species spread throughout the world. Through this the animal world is brought close to human beings, but, at the same time, human beings are elevated above the animal kingdom because they are the bearer of their spirit.

If one teaches in this way and possesses unbiased knowledge of the human being, one will see that such lessons about plants affect the living world of ideas and, through wisdom, people will rightly stand in the world. Through wise intelligence they will be made competent so they assimilate such an enlivened, spirit-endowed view of their position in relation to the whole animal kingdom, which will especially strengthen the will-nature.

One must realize that what I have discussed only for the past twenty minutes must be implemented in teaching children over a longer period of time. Instruction must go from one level to the next so that the children gradually become accustomed to uniting their whole being with such ideas. In this way, these ideas are incorporated into children's will-nature which determines how they position themselves on the Earth. People develop inner strength of will if, in this way, through their own knowledge, they see themselves growing forth from out of the coalescence of all the animal fragments by virtue of the living spirit which brings about this synthesis in the human being. This penetrates into the will-forming aspect of the soul. That is how, through our instruction, we not only bring knowledge about plants and animals, we also affect the building of children's character and of the whole human being by introducing them to the plants so that their wisdom and intelligence is developed in the right way and by introducing them to the animals so that their will is developed in the right way.

Between ages 9 and 12, we will have succeeded in achieving the goal of connecting children with the other creatures, the plants and animals of the Earth, in such a way that—through their intelligence, their wise intelligence, and, on the other side, through an appropriate strength of will for their position in the world and the securing of their own consciousness—they will find their way through the world.

Above all, this is what we should bring about through education: Young people should develop in such a way that they find their path through the world by orienting themselves to both of these aspects. From out of the life of feeling that we have developed in children between ages 7 and 9 or 9½, we have developed their wise intelligence and strength of will. Something that is often completely inorganically developed now comes into the right relationship in the right way: thinking, feeling, and willing. Everything else is rooted in feeling. This must also be understood in relation to children. From out of the feeling-nature we develop thinking in relation to the world of plants, something that will never allow their thinking to become deadened. The will is developed by that which, when viewed correctly, brings children into a connection with the animal kingdom in the right way, but also raises them above the animal kingdom. The study of animals enables the development of the will.

## GA 307, August 15, 1923, Page 193f.

From my remarks on the characteristics of instruction about natural history, plants, and animals, you will, I believe, have realized how in Waldorf education we attempt to tailor the teaching method and the curriculum completely to the developmental principles and forces present in children at various age levels.

We must understand clearly that between ages 9 and 10 children go through an important life transition that I have characterized from various angles. Today I would like to make special note of the fact that between ages 9 and 10 children actually begin to differentiate from the world. Before this time, their views and perceptions made no distinction between the things of the world and their own self. For this reason, up to about age 9 it is necessary, when talking about things of the world like plants, animals, mountains, and rivers, to speak in such a way that it sounds like a fairytale and you appeal primarily to the imagination. Plants, mountains, and rivers talk in such a way that children recognize them as the same kinds of beings that they know themselves to be, in a manner of speaking; the same types of beings echo back to them from the outside world.

If you keep in mind how one should transition into the study of plants and animals at this point in time, you will see that it is a matter of introducing these two kingdoms of nature correctly in order to bring the children into an appropriate relationship with the things of the world.

Children learn about plants in relationship to the Earth. In this way, they absolutely accept that the plants and soil belong together. The Earth becomes a living being from out of which the plants sprout like human hair growth. Of course, the principle of vitality that drives this process is much more lively and richer in form for plants than for human hair. Through this approach, from the very beginning, children are guided into a relationship with the plant world, and the whole Earth, which stimulates the inner being, the soul, and also the physical life of the senses.

If we then teach about the animals so that, in a manner of speaking, we see the human being as an aggregation of all the animal species spread over the Earth like a fan, children will put themselves into a right relationship with the other living beings on the Earth.

By teaching natural history in this way up to a point between ages 11 and 12, you will see that it is completely a matter of always keeping in mind the relationship of human beings to the world.

Now comes the age when children may actually begin to look at what is happening in the outside world that does not have to do with human beings. Between ages 11 and 12 is the earliest possibility of teaching about minerals as they appear in rocks and stones. If you teach about the mineral element without putting it in the context of the plants that grow out of the soil, that is, out of the rock, you will completely ruin the inner flexibility of the life of soul. The thing that has no relationship to the human being is the mineral element. We should begin with the mineral element only after children feel they are properly settled into the world and have absorbed that which stands closer to human beings—the plants and animals—into their thinking, feeling, and willing.

The same thing that applies to the study of minerals applies equally to understanding physics and chemistry, as well as the so-called objective connections in history and geography—that is, all those objective subjects that must be looked at as being detached from the human being. The large historical associations which may not be viewed in their relationship to the human being, as I characterized yesterday, must be put off until children are between 11 and 12 years old. Only then can one begin with things that actually have very little to do with the human being.

Children should start school at around age 7, with the change of teeth. Before that time they really do not belong in school. If we are forced to accept them into school before the change of teeth, then, naturally, we will have to make all kinds of compromises. But I will clarify the main points here. When children enter school we teach in such a way that they do not make any distinctions between themselves and the world. When they are between 9 and 10 years old, we introduce something that belongs to the intellect, albeit a flexible and lively intellect: the study of plants; and, something that leads to a strengthening of the will: the study of animals. Lessons in mineralogy, physics and chemistry appeal only to the intellect. Therefore, as a counterbalance, it is necessary to have lessons in art. But you will find that children between ages 11 and 12 are mature enough to intellectually grasp the process that has to be followed in order to understand the connection between cause and effect.

This process must, of course, take place in the study of physics and chemistry. These processes, which must then also transition into the study of astronomy, may not be started any earlier than age 11 or 12. If we begin earlier with describing simple chemical processes like combustion, for instance, the description should be imaginative because the element of imagination should play the more significant role, not the thought process of cause and effect.

Basically, children should learn about the relationship of cause and effect at a point in time between ages 11 and 12. Before this time period, the less one speaks about so-called causality the better; the soul will be stronger and richer for it. In contrast, if we approach children with the concept of causality before age 11 or 12, their soul will become dry and absorb dead ideas, even dead feelings.

**Page 200f.**

It is very good to begin early with foreign languages because, up to the point in time between ages 9 and 10, children still carry within them something that I have described as especially characteristic of the first stage of life from birth up to the change of teeth. During this period children are primarily imitative beings. They learn their mother tongue totally and completely based on the principle of imitation. Without engaging the intellect in any significant way, they learn to internally re-create what they hear as speech.

And, at the same time as they hear the external sounds and tones of the language, children also hear the internal, musical, soul element. The first language is acquired, if I may be allowed the expression, as a fine, subtle habit. It all goes very deep within a person's being.

When children enter school after the change of teeth, language instruction appeals more to the soul aspect and no longer so strongly to the physical aspect. Nevertheless, up to age 9 or 10, children still bring us enough imaginative, imitative ability for us to teach language in such a way that it is absorbed by the whole being, not just the soul-spiritual forces.

For this reason it is of enormous, far-reaching importance to not let the first three years of primary school go by without instruction in foreign languages. Based upon the human principles of the Waldorf method of education, we begin to teach foreign languages as soon as children enter primary school.

**Page 202f.**

Between ages 9 and 10 children go from consciousness to self-consciousness. They differentiate their own self from the world. This is also the point in time when one, albeit in an unobtrusive way, can transition into rules of grammar and syntax because this is when children start to think about the world and also contemplate a little about themselves. This self-contemplation means that language is no longer merely instinctive, but that logical rules can now be applied to it. Let me make this very clear: Learning a language without any grammar at all is absurd. If one rejects all rules, then one has not given children the inner stability they need in life.

Most importantly, what must be considered is that when children reach the age between 9 and 10, they desire to go from mere consciousness to self-consciousness; therefore any grammar lessons before this time are useless and absurd. One must find this transition between ages 9 and 10 so that one can logically, but almost imperceptibly, move the language instruction from something purely instinctive and imitative into the inclusion of rules of grammar.

This also must be the case with the native language. If one tries to fill children with rules of grammar and syntax before this important moment in their life, one will completely ruin their life of soul. Until that time, language instruction should appeal to children's instinctive, habitual, imitative nature. Their consciousness of self should lead them into language. Normally, consciousness of self and grammar and syntax always go together, between ages 9 and 10. If you keep these things in mind, you will see how the Waldorf method uses the two or three years before this period of time between ages 9 and 10 to rightly incorporate formal language instruction into the curriculum according to childhood phases of development. Step by step, you will see how the

Waldorf method of education teaches the teacher to read, not books, nor some educational system, but rather, Waldorf education teaches the teacher to read human beings.

**Page 206f.**

If we develop a sense of gratitude and love in children before they are 10 years old, we will be able to develop in them a sense of responsibility, or duty, as we call it, in the right way. A sense of responsibility that is developed too early through commands and orders does not lead to any kind of internal religious sense. Most importantly, we must develop gratitude and love in children. Then ethical-moral values, as well as religious values, will develop in the right way. Those who wish to educate in the Christian sense, in the deepest meaning of the word, will need to see to it that what took place before the world at the Mystery of Golgotha, and everything having to do with the personality and divinity of Christ Jesus, is not put before children's souls in a realistic way before they reach age 9–10. One is exposing them to great dangers if they have not been introduced to the idea of universal divinity before this time period. In other words, the Divine Father Principle shows how everywhere we look in nature, in the rocks, but also in the hearts of people, in everything they do for us, we see that the Divine Principle lives everywhere in everything. This universal divinity must be perceived in gratitude and, through a teacher's natural authority, children must be sensitively taught, with love. Then, we have prepared children to take the right attitude toward the Mystery of Golgotha when they are between 9 and 10 years old.

Hence, it is infinitely important to learn to understand human beings in regard to their temporal development. Try to be clear in your mind what a difference there is between teaching 7- or 8-year-old children something from the New Testament or waiting until they are between 9 and 10 years old to develop knowledge of the New Testament for what it is, after we have already stimulated consciousness of the universal divine principle that exists in every being in nature. In the latter instance, one has prepared children for the New Testament in the right way, and they can become acquainted with the completely transcendent glory that is contained in the Gospels. If you approach children with the New Testament too early, it will remain as mere words, a rigid, dry concept, because it will not be able to engage the whole human being. In that case there is a danger that children will become hardened toward anything religious and they will carry that as a hardened element within throughout their lives, instead of in a living way as something that permeates all their perceptions of the world.

This is also the aim of the non-denominational Christian religious instruction given at the Waldorf school to an ever-increasing number of children whose parents wish it. The teaching is based upon a purely human element, and we have also clothed it in a kind of ritual. A "Sunday atmosphere" is created for the children who attend this religious service. When they are dismissed from school, this religious ritual is transformed through a kind of metamorphosis within. Thus, a certain ritual, that is actually similar in many respects to a Catholic Mass, but always appropriate for the age of a child, is associated with life in the Waldorf school which is supported by this non-denominational religious instruction.

## GA 309, April 17, 1924, Page 74ff.

If one follows this period in children's lives from the change of teeth to puberty, which is most decisive for their education, one sees that it is further divided into single, I would say, sub-stages. Up to around age 9 children are not able to clearly differentiate from the environment. That is, they cannot even emotionally perceive any clear difference between feelings for the world and feelings for their own "I." In our times this relationship is not always viewed correctly. If a child who has run into the corner of a table proceeds to hit the table, today's observer would say that the child thinks of the table as a living thing—the cultural-historical term is "animism"—and because the child assumes that the table is a living thing, the child hits the table.

In reality, this is not the case. If one looks into a child's soul, one will find that a child does not see the table as a living thing, but rather, he or she views it the same as arms and hands, simply as parts of his or her being. Children do not yet differentiate between their own self and the world. They do not even see truly living things in the same way as must happen at a later stage in their lives. Things that occur on the outside are seen simply as continuations of a child's own being. And so, I would say, for the first third of the life stage between the change of teeth and puberty, the curriculum must be thoroughly attuned to teaching everything in the form of fairytales, stories, fables, and legends so that children see something in all they are taught that does not separate them from it; that is only a continuation of their own being.

In contrast, there is an important period of development between ages 9 and 10. This phase arrives a little earlier for one child and a little later for another; but it is of the utmost importance. One will notice that children become a little restless, approach a teacher with questioning eyes and expect an answer from the authority figure. They ask questions that can be astonishing in comparison to questions they asked earlier, or perhaps did not ask. They come into a very peculiar internal place. Above all, it is a matter of not pedantically giving all kinds of admonitions or warnings, but rather, feeling your way into the child's mind and putting yourself in his or her place in an empathetic way.

There is something in a child's subconscious at this age that can be characterized like this: Up to this point, whatever a teacher, as the child's respected authority figure, held to be true, good, and beautiful was absolutely what the child also accepted as true, good, and beautiful. Children are naturally devoted to authority. In this period, between ages 9 and 10, something comes over them whereby, dreamlike, a completely undefined question arises: Where does the teacher get all this? Where does it come from? Is the teacher really representative of the world? Of course, the children do not have these specific thoughts because they are not yet able to intellectualize things, but these questions arise in the feeling-nature. Up to this time the teacher was absolutely the child's world; now this feeling arises: Doesn't the world go above and beyond the teacher? While before, a teacher's soul was transparent and children saw into the world through a teacher, now things become more and more opaque and non-transparent and the children ask, by way of a feeling, why something is justified. One must tactfully go about discovering what is right for each child. It is not really a matter of having prepared words to say, but rather, through inner tactfulness, one should know how to adapt to each situation as it arises. If at this time a teacher finds the right approach, through empathy, it will have enormous significance for the rest of a person's life. If, during these internal life situations, children find in a teacher a person about whom they have the feeling that they are clarifying mysteries of the world, it becomes more and more valuable over time. This definitely belongs in the Waldorf education method and didactics.

At this point in time children learn to differentiate from the world. Therefore, one can now transition from the study of plants, which I demonstrated yesterday, to the study of animals. If you approach teaching in the way I have explained, you will find you are appropriately meeting the feelings children have for the world.

**Page 84f.**

Before age 9 or 10 children cannot yet differentiate between the world and their "I." They will also not be able to write sentences on their own. At the most, children will be able to reproduce what they have been told in the form of fairytales, legends, or other stories. Only after age 9 or 10 can one slowly begin to approach children with images and thoughts which they can then write down in their own words. But the inner thought structure that is necessary in order to transition into sentence writing is really only there beginning around age 12. If you begin the transition to sentence writing too early, I guarantee that, although you may not bring children into a condition of sclerosis of the soul, you will cause a kind of rickets of the soul that will lead to inner incompetence and weakness in later life.

**GA 310, July 20, 1924, Page 80ff.**

If you advance the lessons in the other subjects which must be taught along the lines of the viewpoints that have arisen from our considerations here, you will come to realize that you should also teach history and geography, for example, through the use of pictorial imagery because at this age children are able to take in only that which is presented pictorially, through the feeling-nature. History must be described pictorially. We must paint and model with our words! This develops a child's mind, because, above all, what does not yet live in a child in the first two phases of the second seven-year epoch between the change of teeth and puberty is what we call the concept of causality. Before age 7 children really should not be in school. If you take the time period from ages 7 to $9\frac{1}{3}$, you have the first subdivision of the second seven-year epoch; from ages $9\frac{1}{3}$ to $11\frac{2}{3}$, you have the second subdivision; from ages $11\frac{2}{3}$ to about age 14, you have the third subdivision.

In the first subdivision of the second seven-year epoch the children are completely oriented toward the pictorial. We must speak in the manner of fairytales, and everything in the outside world must remain undifferentiated from children's own nature. Plants must talk to each other; a mineral talks to another mineral; plants must give each other a kiss and have mothers and fathers, and so on. When this point in time has been reached, that is from age 9½ forward, a child's "I" will begin to separate from the outside world. Then one can begin to approach children with knowledge of the plants and animals in a more realistic way. However, during the first few years of life, one will always teach history subjects in the manner of fairytales and legends.

In the second subdivision of the longer seven-year epoch, that is, from ages 9⅓ to 11⅔, one will continue to speak pictorially. And only when children are close to age 12 can they be approached with things under the sway of the concept of causality, which goes a little bit into abstract concepts whereby cause and effect can enter into it. Before this time children are as unapproachable with the concept of cause and effect as a colorblind person is to color. As a teacher, sometimes one has no idea how unnecessary it is to talk about cause and effect. The scientific viewpoint about things that we are so accustomed to today cannot be discussed with children until after age 12.

This also requires that we wait until around age 12 before teaching anything that has to do with something non-living where the concept of causality would come into play. In teaching history, we must also wait until about this age before transitioning from a pictorial presentation to one which addresses cause and effect, whereby the causes underlying historical events are sought. Before this, one should be concerned only with what can be brought to children as living things with soul qualities.

## GA 311, August 14, 1924, Page 43ff.

When children reach the age between 9 and 10, they are able to differentiate from the environment. The difference between subject and object—subject = oneself, object = the other—in reality, begins to appear at this point in time. We can then begin to talk about outside things, whereas before we had to treat outside things as if they were actually one with a child's own body. Yesterday I said that we should treat outside things as if they talk and act like people. Through this children get the impression that the outside world is simply a continuation of their own being.

After children have reached the age of 9 or 10, it is a matter of introducing them to a few elementary facts, the essence of the outside world. We must introduce them to the plant and animal kingdoms.

I will speak later about other subjects, but with these two things in particular, we must see to it that we introduce children to them in the way their developing human nature demands.

The first thing we must do in this regard is to throw out all textbooks. The way textbooks are created these days they contain nothing on the subject of plants and animals that one can actually teach. These textbooks of today are good for teaching adults about plants and animals, but we ruin the individuality of a child if we use them in our schools. Textbooks and handbooks that come with instructions on how they are to be used in the classroom really do not exist today. That is to say, it is a matter of the following:

If you put an individual plant in front of children and demonstrate this or that using that plant, you have done something that has no connection to reality. A single plant, in and of itself, has no reality. If you pull out a hair from your head and look at it as if it were something in and of itself, it has no reality. In ordinary life we say of everything that we can see with our eyes that it is real; it has a reality. But there is a difference between looking at a rock and forming some opinion about it, or looking at a hair, or a rose. After ten years the rock will still be the same as it is today, but after two days the rose will not be the same. A rose is only a reality when it is connected to a rosebush. A hair has no reality in and of itself but is only a reality in connection with the head of the whole body. If one goes out into the fields and rips plants out of the ground, it is as if one had plucked out the hair of the Earth. Plants belong in the soil exactly like hair belongs to the human organism. To look at a hair by itself, as if it could somehow grow and exist by itself, is nonsense.

It makes just as little sense to fill a jar with plants and take them home to examine them one by one. This has nothing to do with reality, and it is not possible in this way to gain correct knowledge about nature and humankind.

Here we have a plant (see top drawing), but this alone is not a plant. The earth beneath it also belongs in the picture. There are plants

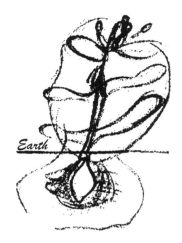

that spread their roots a very great distance in the ground.

The way you can teach that the bit of soil in which the plant is rooted belongs to the plant in a wide radius is by showing that by putting a little natural fertilizer in the ground the plant will grow better. It is not only the plant that lives, but also the surrounding soil lives along with it.

There are plants that bloom in the spring around May or June and produce fruit in the autumn. Then they wilt and die. They remain in the soil because they belong together. But there are other plants that take the energy of the soil from out of their surroundings (see drawing below). The root takes up into itself the energy in the surrounding soil. Because the roots have now taken the energy into themselves, the life energy of the soil rises up and the result is a tree.

What is a tree, exactly? A tree is a colony made up of many plants. Whether you have a hill that is only partially alive with many plants on it or you have a tree trunk which has drawn into itself a much more

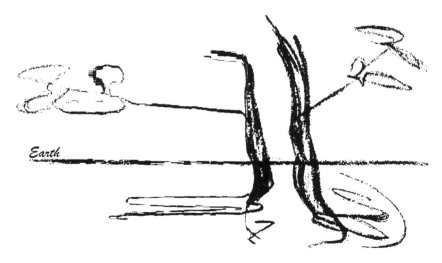

vital, lively force of the soil, it makes no difference. You can absolutely not objectively, factually, realistically examine a plant just by itself.

**Page 54**

I told you that between ages 9 and 10 children get to the point that they differentiate between their own "I" as subject and the outside world as object. Children differentiate from the environment. Earlier, one was able to tell only fairytales and legends in which the rocks and plants talked and acted like people. At that time children did not yet differentiate from the environment. Now, when they begin to make the distinction, we must again connect them with the environment, but at a higher level. We must show them that the ground they stand upon, as a natural matter of course, belongs together with its plants. Then children will start to develop a practical sense, just as I have shown you, also for agriculture. They will know that, in a manner of speaking, natural fertilizer is used because certain plants need the soil beneath to be alive. Children will not see a single plant as being something in and of itself and they will not see an animal that way either. They will look upon the animal kingdom as a very great analysis of the human being that is spread out over the Earth in all its different parts. Thus children get to know where they stand upon the Earth, and they also know where the animal kingdom stands in relationship to them.

It is of enormous importance that, from age 10 to about age 12, we awaken this notion of plant-earth and animal-human being. In this way children place themselves with their whole being—body, soul, and spirit—into the world in a very particular way.

Through the fact that we teach children to develop a feeling (and this must all be brought artistically, through the feeling-nature) for how plants and earth belong together, they will become wise and brightly clever; they will think naturally. Through the fact that we try to teach children how they stand in relation to animals (even though it is only in the classroom, you will see that they grasp this concept)—the will forces of all animals live within the human being, differentiated and with the appropriate individualization, all the characteristics, all the feeling of form that is developed in animals, live in the human being —in this way they will position themselves into the world naturally, according to the nature of their own being. Human beings receive will-impulses through this knowledge.

## GA 311, August 15, 1924, Page 70

For the time being it is not important that children commit such a story to memory. At this age, between the change of teeth and age 9 or 10, what I am now speaking about hardly comes into question; it is even better if one counts on the children remembering what they can remember and what they forget, just let it be forgotten. Memory training can be accomplished by way of subjects other than story-telling, as I will explain.

## GA 311, August 18, 1924, Page 108ff.

Different things are expressed in different languages. If one wished to designate the same thing, an American and an Italian would both say "Kopf." But they do not designate the same thing. In the primordial languages, or protolanguages, of human beings everything had a uniform designation. Therefore, the human protolanguage was the same for everyone. Then people began to separate and they expressed things differently. That is how all the different words originated. If one designates different things as "the same," then one can no longer feel what is contained within them. It is very important that one not drive out the feeling for language; that must remain. For this reason one may not allow a formal study of language before age 9 or 10.

Only then can one transition into defining nouns, adjectives, verbs, adverbs, and so on—not before ages 9 or 10. Otherwise you will be examining something outside of children that is actually still a part of them. And this they cannot grasp because they cannot yet differentiate between their own self and the environment. It is very important that you keep this in mind: Nothing of grammar or any language comparisons before children are 9 or 10! Then they will receive something through speech that is similar to what they receive through singing.

This feeling of inner well-being one gets through singing can be illustrated by thinking of it as similar to the feeling of well-being a cow has rising from her digestive organs when she is grazing on a meadow. Just such an inner feeling of well-being must be present, or at least a feeling for the thing itself, so that children feel what is contained in a word and the internal "motion." Language must be experienced internally and not just thought about by the head. Today most people "think" language with only their head. If they want to know what is correct in one language, how something is translated from one language to another, they simply look it up in a dictionary. The words are all nicely arranged so that the German word "Kopf" stands for the English word "head." And so, the feeling takes hold that these two things are the same. But they are not the same. There is always a slight difference in the designation. That difference can be expressed only from out of feeling. It is important to take this into consideration when teaching languages.

In addition, there is another spiritual element that comes into play. When someone dies or a person comes down to Earth, he or she has, for instance, no possibility of understanding the so-called substantives in a language. The so-called dead know nothing about nouns. All the things here that have names, the dead know nothing about them. But they still know something about properties. That is to say, one has the possibility of communicating with the dead by way of qualities and characteristics.

But this also soon ceases to be the case. The most enduring communication will be through the use of verbs, action words, in the active and passive voices, and the most lingering of all, through emotions, expressed as, for example, "Oh!" or "Ah!" or "Ugh!" These interjections are preserved the longest of all by the dead.

From this you can see how human souls are dependent upon living within the interjections if they are not to become completely unspiritual. All interjections are vowels. The consonants, which, in any case, are very soon lost after death, or were not present before the descent to Earth, are imitations of that which is external. We must truly experience this in our feelings and look to see where children are with this and not drive it out by teaching about nouns, adjectives, etc., too early but actually begin only when they are 9 or 10 years old.

## GA 311, August 19, 1924, Page 116

If you take the physical development of children from birth to the change of teeth, you will see that it is the head organization, the nerve-sense organization that is especially active here. In the first period of life, children develop physically from the head downward. You must be able to see this clearly. First, take a look at a human embryo, that is, a child that is yet unborn. The head is enormous. Everything else is still somewhat shriveled. Then the child is born. The infant's head is still the most prominent external feature, and growth and everything proceeds from out of the head. For children between ages 7 and 14, this is no longer the case. Breathing rhythm, the rhythm of blood circulation, the whole rhythmic system is what predominates between the change of teeth and puberty, only rhythm!

But how is it with rhythm? If I have a lot of thinking to do, that is to say, if I have to study a great deal, I become tired; my head gets tired. If I have to walk a lot and strain my limbs, I also get tired. Our head system, our nerve-sense system, and our metabolic-limb system can all become tired, but our rhythmic system can never become tired. Just think about it: You must breathe all day long. Your heart beats all night and will never stop from birth to death. It must beat in rhythm continuously. It will absolutely never become tired.

In education and teaching, you must address the system that controls human beings. That is to say, between the change of teeth and puberty, you must appeal to the rhythmic system through pictures and images. Everything you do or say must be said or done in such a way that the head takes part as little as possible but the heart, the whole rhythmic system, is completely engaged. What is the result? During such lessons children will absolutely not become tired because one has engaged the rhythmic system and not the head.

**Page 118**

For children of primary school age, we must see to it that we appeal only to the rhythmic system. And this rhythmic system, which never tires and is never over-exerted, if we engage it in the right way, the intellectual element is really not needed, but only the pictorial, and that which stems from the imagination. Therefore, you must unfailingly allow the faculty of imagination to hold sway in the classroom. Even in the last years of elementary school, from ages $11^{2}/_{3}$ to 14, even then, you should make what is dead come alive through imagination and tie it in with life! It is absolutely possible to connect all physical phenomena with life; one must only possess imagination; that is the only thing necessary.

Further, it will be a question of allowing this imagination faculty to prevail over the writing of compositions when children are assigned to write something they have come up with themselves. Here, it is a matter of not assigning a composition without first thoroughly discussing it so they are familiar with the subject. As the teacher, you should talk about the subject of the composition from your own knowledge previously obtained. Then, having been informed about the subject, children should create their composition. You must not deviate from this approach even in the last years before puberty. Even then you should not allow children to simply write whatever occurs to them. There should be nothing in the composition that does not maintain the mood that was called forth during discussion of the subject. Here also a kind of liveliness must prevail. A teacher's liveliness of spirit must cross over to the children's liveliness of spirit.

# Bibliography

*GA – Gesamtausgabe (Complete Works)*
*\*English translation available at www.rsarchive.org*

GA 77a    The Duty of Anthroposophy to Life and Science

GA 84    What Is the Purpose of the Goetheanum and
Anthroposophy?

GA 150    World of the Spirit and Its Projection into the Physical
Being – The Influence of the Dead on the World of the
Living

GA 194*    The Mission of Michael:
The Revelation of the Actual Mystery of the Human Being

GA 206    On Becoming a Human Being, World Soul and World
Spirit – Part II: The Human Being as a Spiritual Being in
Historical Evolution

GA 212*    The Human Soul in Relation to World Evolution

GA 217*    The Younger Generation

GA 218*    Planetary Spheres and Their Influence on Man's Life on
Earth and in the Spiritual Worlds

GA 232*    Mystery Centers

GA 294*    Practical Course for Teachers: Method (II)

GA 295    Practical Course for Teachers: Discussion and Curriculum
(III)

GA 297    The Waldorf School in Concept and Practice

GA 297a   Education for Life, Self-Education, and Educational
          Practice

GA 300    Conferences with Teachers at the Free Waldorf School
          from 1919 to 1924

GA 301    The Renewal of the Educational Arts through Spiritual
          Science

GA 302    Knowledge of the Human Being as it Relates to Designing
          a Curriculum

GA 303    The Healthy Development of a Human Being – An
          Introduction to Anthroposophical Education and Method

GA 304    Educational Method on the Basis of Anthroposophy

GA 304a   Anthroposophical Study of the Human Being and
          Education

GA 305*   Spiritual Ground of Education – Spiritual Values in
          Education and Social Life

GA 306    Educational Practice from the Viewpoint of Spiritual
          Science-Based Knowledge of the Human Being – Educating
          Children and Adolescents

GA 307*   Education: Spiritual Life of the Present and Education

GA 308    Teaching Method and the Requisite Conditions for
          Education

GA 309    Anthroposophical Education and its Prerequisites

GA 310*   Human Values in Education

GA 311*   The Kingdom of Childhood

GA 313*   Anthroposophical Spiritual Science and Medical Therapy

# Index

# M

memory 10, 14, 19, 33-34, 37, 56, 81, 103, 135, 177

mineralogy 13, 127, 165

moral 9, 16, 18-19, 21, 28, 32, 39, 53-57, 70, 81, 83-85, 88-90, 93-94,
116-117, 119, 148, 168

mother tongue 144, 166

movement 41, 44-46, 57-58, 71, 78, 106, 135, 154, 160

muscle, muscle system 7, 42-43, 45-47

music, musical 7-8, 42-44, 58-59, 65, 71, 121, 126, 151, 166

# N

natural history 11, 12, 21, 87, 89, 109-110, 112, 119, 121, 123, 125-126,
134, 150, 153, 163-164

nature, study of nature 6, 9-11, 21, 25, 30-33, 36, 40, 49, 64-65, 68, 85, 87,
89, 98, 102, 110, 115, 117-122, 124, 128, 136, 143, 146, 151, 154-155,
158-159, 164, 168, 174

# P

parents 31, 77, 100, 169

physics 10, 13, 35, 75, 98, 125, 127, 147, 151, 165

physiognomy 7, 30, 41, 103, 104

pictorial 13, 24, 34, 58, 61, 63-64, 71-72, 83, 91, 98, 100, 104, 106-107, 151,
155, 159, 172-173, 180

plants, plant kingdom, study of plants 12-14, 17, 31, 35, 39, 60-62, 65, 72,
84-86, 91, 100, 106, 109, 121, 126, 133-135, 138, 142-144, 146-147,
151-157, 159, 162-165, 171-176

puberty 5, 22-23, 27-28, 34, 43, 50, 58, 66, 71, 73-76, 83-85, 89, 97, 104,
122, 137, 147-148, 150, 154-155, 169-170, 172, 179-180

# R

read, reading 37, 59, 93, 123, 126, 142, 155, 158-160, 168

religion, religious instruction 2, 6, 11, 15, 32, 39, 40, 56, 63, 69, 70, 82,
93-94, 97, 127-128, 168-169

respiration 58, 80

reverence 2, 9, 15-16, 19, 56, 63, 69-70, 92-96

Rubicon 6-7, 9, 15-17, 34, 36, 49, 90, 93, 110, 118, 123

# S

sclerosis 10, 103, 172

self-awareness, consciousness of self 11, 118, 126, 145, 167

sense of beauty 12, 135, 137

18297388R00113

Printed in Poland
by Amazon Fulfillment
Poland Sp. z o.o., Wrocław